The Pilgrim's Progress Part 2 Christiana's Journey

A Readable Modern-Day Version of John Bunyan's
The Pilgrim's Progress Part 2

Book by John Bunyan

Revision by Alan Vermilye

BROWN CHAIR BOOKS
BOOKS THAT INSPIRE

The Pilgrim's Progress, Part 2 Christiana's Journey
A Readable, Modern-Day Version of John Bunyan's Pilgrim's Progress Part 2

Copyright © 2023 Alan Vermilye
Brown Chair Books

ISBN-13 Paperback: 978-1-948481-35-9
ISBN-13 Hardbackback: 978-1-948481-31-1

To learn more about this book and the Bible study resources that go with it, to order additional copies, or to download the answer guide, visit www.BrownChairBooks.com.

No part of this work may be reproduced or transmitted in any form or by any means, electronic or mechanical, including photocopying and recording, or by any information storage or retrieval system, except as may be expressly permitted by the 1976 Copyright Act in writing from the publisher.

All rights reserved.
Version 1

Contents

The Study Guide	V
Author's Introduction	VII
Introduction	IX
1. Mr. Sagacity	1
2. Christiana and Her Boys	5
3. A Conversation with Mrs. Nervousness	11
4. The Wicket Gate	17
5. Intercession for Mercy	22
6. Distracted from Danger	28
7. The Interpreter's House	33
8. Great Heart Leads the Women	42
9. The Consequences of the Cross	47
10. Following the Path of Christian	52
11. An Encounter with Grim	57
12. Arrival at the Palace Beautiful	61
13. Prudence Talks to the Boys About Faith	67
14. Mr. Brisk Visits Mercy	71
15. Matthew Falls Sick	74
16. Leaving the Palace Beautiful	79

17.	The Valley of Humiliation	83
18.	The Valley of the Shadow of Death	89
19.	Old Honest and Mr. Fearing	96
20.	Mr. Self Will	107
21.	Welcomed by Gaius	112
22.	Slay Good and Mr. Feeble Mind	122
23.	Good Samaritan's Promise	126
24.	The Church in Vanity	131
25.	Storming Doubting Castle	139
26.	The View From the Mountains	145
27.	Valiant's Zeal for Truth	151
28.	The Enchanted Ground	159
29.	The Land of Beulah	168
30.	The Pilgrims Receive a Summons	173

The Bible Study Guide

The Pilgrim's Progress Part 2 Study Guide is a 6-week Bible study created specifically for this book.

Perfect for small groups or individual study, each weekly study session applies a biblical framework to the concepts found in each chapter of the book. Although intriguing and entertaining, much of Bunyan's writings can be difficult to grasp.

The Pilgrim's Progress Part 2 Study Guide will guide you to a better understanding of the key concepts of the book, the supporting Bible passages, and the relevance to our world today. Each study question is ideal for group discussion, and answers to each question are available online.

You will also find commentary, character and places summaries, discussion questions for each section, and complete answers to all questions available for free online.

You can find retailers in order to purchase this book at www.BrownChairBooks.com.

Author's Introduction

I can honestly say that I never would have imagined just how popular my earnest rendering of John Bunyan's *The Pilgrim's Progress* would become. In just under three years, the book has received over 2,200 reviews and is an Amazon Best Seller on most days.

But more than that, I've received many encouraging emails from so many people of all ages and around the world who have read the book and can finally understand it. Then I hear of how reading it affected their faith, giving them a new outlook on their Christian walk. I couldn't be more humbled and grateful for all those experiences and give God all the glory.

Almost immediately after publication, I also had many requests to write the second book in the series, which details the journey of Christian's wife, Christiana, and her boys to the Celestial City. But I really wanted to first tackle the third in the series, titled *The Life and Death of Mr. Badman*. Unbeknownst to me, Bunyan actually wrote this story prior to the story of Christiana then returned to the second story in the series.

Well, after publishing *The Life and Death of Mr. Badman*, I, too, immediately set my sights back on the second half of this amazing story.

As with the previous two, my most important consideration was to convert the antiquated text into simple, conversational English without being unfaithful to Bunyan's original text. In fact, if you compare my version with the original, you will find no key element missing. I also kept the original scriptural references included by Bunyan.

If you've not read the first in *The Pilgrim's Progress* series featuring the story of Christian, I would suggest doing so before reading this book. Bunyan does a masterful job of weaving details from Christian's journey in the first book into Christiana's story as she follows the same path to the Celestial City. In fact, Bunyan goes further by providing additional details of Christian's various encounters that are not included in the first book, which I think you'll find very interesting.

I'm so glad to have completed the series, and I look forward to hearing from you. Please drop me a note at www.BrownChairBooks.com. I would love to hear about your experience with the book.

God bless, and enjoy the book!

Alan

Introduction

My Dear Friend,

It's been some time since I told you about my dream of Christian the pilgrim and of his dangerous journey to the Celestial City. It was good for me to tell you the story, but I also believe it was beneficial to you. If you recall, it was in this story that I told you about his wife and children and the fact that they refused to go with him on his journey. Christian, though, feared that if he stayed in the City of Destruction, he would be destroyed, and since he didn't dare run that risk, he felt compelled to go on without them. As I mentioned to you before, this was the reason he left his family and went on his way.

I've been wanting to report back to you with an update about those whom he left behind. Unfortunately, I've been incredibly busy lately and unable to make my normal trips to those places where Christian went. It's been only recently that I've had business in the area, providing the perfect opportunity to make further inquiries. So, once again, I headed down to the city, stopping in some woods about a mile outside of it, where I laid down to sleep. It was there that I dreamed again.

In my dream, an older gentleman came to where I was lying. He introduced himself as Mr. Sagacity, and since we were heading in the same direction, I suggested we travel together. As we began our journey, talking as traveling companions normally do, our discussion naturally led to Christian and all that had happened on his journey. Following is an account of our conversation.

Chapter One

Mr. Sagacity

As we continued traveling along the road, walking at a steady pace, I noticed a town on the lefthand side of the road. I pointed ahead, asking him, "Sir, do you know what town that is?"

"It's the City of Destruction," the old man said without hesitation. "The town's population is quite large, but its residents are not well and are very lazy."

Memories of a time not so long ago flooded my mind. "I thought that was the city," I replied. "I once visited the town myself, so I know what you say about it is true."

"Very true!" Sagacity nodded and sighed in disgust. "I only wish I could speak a better truth about the people who live there."

"Well, sir," I said, narrowing my eyes in on him, "it's clear to me you're an honest man, one who enjoys listening to and talking about good things. Tell me, did you ever hear the story about a man named Christian who lived in this town some time back? He went on a journey up toward the higher regions."

"Hear of him?" Sagacity bellowed, whirling around to face me. "Of course I've heard of him! And I've also heard of the difficulties, troubles, wars, captivities, cries, groans, horrors, and fears that he encountered along his journey. Not only that but

I assure you that our entire country talks about his exploits. There are probably not more than a few people in the entire city who've not heard about Christian and his adventures. In fact, I believe most people are quite familiar with the account of his dangerous journey. It's no doubt garnered him many an adoring fan."

He then paused, as if choosing his next words carefully. "Of course, you must understand," he said slowly, eyebrows raised, "that when he lived here, almost everyone thought he was a fool. But now everyone considers him brave for living where he does and would love to have all he received because of his journey. Few people, though, are resolved enough to run the same risks that he did," he said, shaking his head sadly.

I nodded in agreement. "Well, they're absolutely correct in saying that he's living well now considering he lives at the Fountain of Life! And he has it all with no work or sorrow because there's none of that where he is. Tell me, what do the people say about him?"

"Well, I'll tell you what they say!" Sagacity replied eagerly, as if he had already prepared his answer. "Why, they say all kinds of strange things about him. Some say he now walks in white with a gold chain around his neck and a crown of gold inlaid with pearls on his head.[1] Others say that the angels who sometimes revealed themselves to him on his journey are now his friends and that he's as familiar with them there in the higher regions as one neighbor might be with another here.

"Then there are others who confidently believe that the King of the place where he is has already given him a very grand and pleasant place to live. Each day, they say, he eats, drinks, and walks with the King, receiving the smiles and favor of the One who is judge over all that is there."[2]

Sagacity paused, only to catch his breath. "Not only that but many expect that his Prince—the Lord of that country who has become very fond of Christian—will come into these parts soon.

He will want Christian's neighbors to explain their reason, if they can, why they thought so little of him for becoming a pilgrim and why they scorned and ridiculed him.[3] It's also said that His Majesty is so concerned with the wrongs that were committed against Christian when he became a pilgrim that He views all those offenses as if they committed the acts against Him.[4] But that's really no surprise," the old man said with a wave of the hand. "It was because of the love Christian had for his Prince that he ventured out to begin with."

"Well, I'm certainly glad to hear of this!" I said excitedly. "Obviously I'm glad for Christian's sake, the poor man, because now he gets to rest from his work. He's now reaping the benefits of all his tears that have turned into joy since he's beyond the gunshot of his enemies and out of reach of those who hate him.[5] But it also pleases me to know that rumors of these things are still being discussed in the City of Destruction. Who knows? It just may have a positive impact on some who are left behind."

We walked in silence for a moment before I shifted the conversation. "Please, I must ask while it's still fresh in my mind. Have you heard anything about Christian's wife and children? Poor souls! My thoughts have often wondered what became of them."

Sagacity stopped walking and turned to face me. "Who?" he asked curiously. "Are you referring to Christiana and her sons? Why," he said with a laugh, "they're believed to have done as well as Christian did himself! In the beginning, they were foolish, not at all persuaded by his tears or heartfelt pleas to go with him. Then, amazingly, they had second thoughts and packed up and followed him!"

A smile formed at the corner of my mouth. The story was getting better and better. "Are you sure," I said with a questioning gaze, "that his wife and children have all left the city?"

"Oh yes, absolutely!" Sagacity replied without hesitation. "In fact, I'm thoroughly acquainted with the entire matter since I was there when it happened. I can tell you more if you'd like."

I had no reason to believe he wasn't telling the truth and nodded my assent.

"Great!" Sagacity said, rubbing his hands together. "And I'm confident you'll have no concerns when you share this story with others. I mean, the fact is, they've all left on their journey, both Christian's wonderful wife and their four boys. And since it appears we're going to be traveling together for a while, I can give you an account of the complete story exactly as it happened."

---

1. Revelation 3:4
2. Zechariah 3:7, Luke 14:14–15
3. Jude 14–15
4. Luke 10:16
5. Revelation 14:13, Psalm 126:5–6

Chapter Two

Christiana and Her Boys

Sagacity continued walking as he began his story. It was as if he had told it a hundred times before. There was excitement in his voice and an urgency to share all he knew.

"Christian's wife's name was Christiana—or at least this was her name the day she and her children became pilgrims," he said. "After her husband crossed the river and was never heard from again, she thought about everything that had happened. First she thought about losing her husband and that loving bond between them being utterly broken. For you know," he said, turning to face me, "it's only natural that the living should have many sad thoughts when remembering the loved ones they've lost. And in this case, she shed many tears over losing her husband."

The expression on the old gentleman's face seemed to suggest there was more to Christiana's thoughts than just sadness over her loss.

"Christiana also asked herself whether her rude behavior toward her husband was the reason she no longer saw him. Perhaps that's why he was taken away from her. Questions like these only led to a swarm of more thoughts swirling in her mind—all of which centered on the unkind, insincere, and ungodly treatment she had displayed toward Christian when he was there. As you can imagine, this troubled her conscience and loaded her with guilt.

"This soon led to her recalling her husband's restless groanings, endless tears, and deep sorrow. It left her completely broken. She remembered how she refused to listen to all his pleas and loving encouragement for her and their sons to leave the City of Destruction with him. It all came back to her like a flash of lightening—everything Christian had said and done for her and the boys, all while carrying such a heavy burden. It broke her heart to think about it. What was worse was that she could still hear his distressed and bitter cries ringing out in her ears, saying, 'What should I do to be saved?'

"'She could take it no longer and gathered her children together. 'Sons,' she said to them, 'we're all ruined! I have sinned against your father, and now he's gone. He so desperately wanted us to go with him, but I refused to go myself and, as a result, hindered your opportunity to find true life.'

"The children, after hearing their mother's news, all broke down in tears, crying and expressing their desire to follow their father.

"'Oh,' said Christiana hopelessly, 'if only it had been our destiny to go with him! Then, perhaps, we would be better off than we are now. I once foolishly imagined that your father's troubles came from some ridiculous fancy he had or that depression and sadness had overcome him. But now I cannot rid myself of the thought that it was not some ridiculous fancy but rather originated from another cause. I now believe he received the light of life, which, as I understand it, helped him escape the snares of death.'[1]

"They continued thinking about their husband and father while regretting all they had lost. Their seemingly hopeless situation just led to more tears and cries that filled their house with desperation.

"That next night," the old man continued as his eyebrows drew close together, "Christiana had a dream. In it she saw an enormous book opened before her in which was recorded a summary of everything she had done in this life. As she reflected upon what she saw, suddenly a horrible, dark stain came upon her, and she cried out aloud in her sleep, 'Lord, have mercy on a sinner like me!'[2] And the children heard her.

"After this, still dreaming, she thought she saw two very hideous creatures standing by her bedside. They were saying, 'What should we do with this woman? She's crying out for mercy while awake and asleep. If she's allowed to continue in this manner, we will lose her as we lost her husband. By any means necessary, we must try to distract her from thoughts of the afterlife. If we're unsuccessful, then all the world cannot prevent her from becoming a pilgrim.'

"Immediately, she awoke sweating and trembling, but before long she fell back asleep again. While asleep, she saw her husband, Christian, in a heavenly place among many immortals. He was standing with a harp in his hand playing it before the One who had a rainbow about His head and sat on a throne.

"She also saw her husband bow his head with his face to the ground that was under the Prince's feet. He was saying, 'With all my heart, I thank my Lord and King for bringing me into this place.' Then a great company of those who were standing about shouted and played their harps, but no living man could understand what they said, only Christian and his companions.

"Well, Christiana got up the next morning and, after praying to God, began talking with her children. A short while later, there was a hard knock at the door. She glanced curiously at her children then called out, 'If you're coming in God's name, come in.'

"A man opened the door and greeted them, saying, 'Amen! And may there be peace to those in this house!' He then looked steadily at the children's mother, saying, 'Christiana, do you know why I've come?'

"Her face blushed, and she trembled but said nothing. Her heart, though, felt as if it would pound right out of her chest as she thought, *Where did this man come from and what could he possibly want with me?*

"Her silence was soon answered by this mysterious man. 'My name is Secret,' he explained, 'and I live with those on high, where it's been said that you have a desire to be as well. It's also said you're now aware of the evil you committed toward your husband, including turning your heart against his ways and keeping these children ignorant of the truth.'

"The man paused as if to let this sink in then said, 'Christiana, God, who is full of mercy, sent me here to tell you He's ready to forgive you and delights in pardoning offenses. He also would have you know that you're invited to come into His presence. It's there at His table that He will feed you the best food of His house and with the heritage of Jacob, your father.

"'Your husband, Christian, is there along with a great number more of his friends, all gazing into the face that gives life to those who look upon Him. They will be glad to hear your feet stepping over your Father's threshold.'

"Christiana was ashamed when she heard this and bowed her head to the ground. The visitor, however, proceeded, saying, 'Christiana, I have also brought you a letter from your husband's king.'

"She took the letter and opened it, releasing the most pleasant fragrance found in the best of perfumes.[3] Inside the letter, she found written in gold an invitation from the King to take the same journey that her husband had, for that was the only way to come to His city and to live in His presence with joy forever.

"Overcome with emotion, she cried out to her visitor, 'Sir, will you take me and my children with you so that we also may worship the King?'

"'Christiana,' the visitor said softly, looking deeply into her eyes, 'the bitter comes before the sweet. You must go through the same troubles that your husband did before you can enter the Celestial City. I would advise you to do just like Christian and go to the Wicket Gate, there in the distance,' he said, pointing out the window of the home. 'It's at that gate you'll find yourself at the beginning of your journey. I wish you much success. I would also advise you to put this letter next to your chest and read it often to yourself and to your children until you have it memorized by heart. It's one of the songs you must sing through all the years of your earthly pilgrimage.[4] Then at the end of your journey, you must present this letter at the last gate.'"

Now, in my dream, it seemed the story he told me greatly affected Sagacity, although he pressed on.

"Christiana gathered her children close to her, saying, 'My sons, as you know, my soul has been troubled lately about your father's death. It's not that I doubt his happiness. Far from it! In fact, I'm satisfied that he's now well where he is. But I'm consumed with thoughts about my own spiritual state as well as yours, which I believe, beyond any doubt, is naturally corrupt. The way I treated your father in his own distress has left a significant burden on my conscience. It's because of my lack of compassion that I turned my heart and yours against him, refusing to leave with him on his journey.'

"'Just thinking about what I did would altogether kill me if it weren't for a dream I had last night, not to mention this stranger's encouragement this morning,' she said with a nod toward Secret. 'Come, my children, let's pack up and leave for the gate that leads to the Celestial Country. There we will see your father and be with him and his friends in peace according to the laws of that land.'

"The boys burst into tears of joy because their mother's heart was so willing to leave and take the same journey as their father. Having accomplished his mission, their visitor left, wishing them farewell as the family prepared to set out for their journey."

---

1. James 1:23–25; John 8:12, Proverbs 14:27
2. Luke 18:13
3. Song of Solomon 1:3
4. Psalm 119:54

Chapter Three

A Conversation with Mrs. Nervousness

Mr. Sagacity told the story skillfully, weaving in and out of details with such familiarity that you would have thought the story was his own.

"As they were preparing to leave," he continued, "two neighbor ladies came knocking at the door, and just like before, Christiana called out, 'If you've come in God's name, come in.'

"The women shared equally stunned looks because they were not used to this type of greeting, especially from Christiana. Still, they walked in and were surprised to find her and the boys scurrying around as if leaving on some sort of trip.

"'Christiana, what's the meaning of all this?' they asked, studying her movements carefully.

"Christiana stopped momentarily, turning her attention to the eldest of the two, Mrs. Nervousness. 'I'm preparing to leave on a journey.'

"Mrs. Nervousness was the daughter of the man Christian had met on the Hill of Difficulty and who would've had him go back for fear of the lions. Now appearing a trifle startled herself, she asked, 'What journey? Please tell me where you are going.'

"'I'm following after my husband, Christian.' No sooner had Christiana said her husband's name than she collapsed into a chair next to her, head in her hands, crying.

"'I hope this is not true, Christiana!' Mrs. Nervousness said, casting a quick appraising glance toward the boys. 'Please think about your poor children! Be a good mother, and do not leave them.'

"'Oh, no,' Christiana said, shaking her head while rising from the chair and smoothing out her dress, 'my children are going with me. None of them want to stay behind.'

"Mrs. Nervousness's voice became grim, and her face displayed a disapproving look. 'I can only wonder deep in my heart who or what has placed these thoughts in your mind.'

"Christiana was quick to perceive the inflection in her neighbor's voice. 'Oh, Mrs. Nervousness,' she said and then added with emphasis, 'I know that if you knew as much as I do, you would go with me.'

"'Is that right?' the old woman stammered. 'Well, please share with us what new information has you so worked up and completely out of your mind that you're tempted to leave your neighbors and go...who knows where.'

"Christiana sat back down and stared aimlessly out the window. 'Mrs. Nervousness,' she began softly, 'please understand. It has deeply troubled me since Christian left us but especially since he went over the river. What troubles me the most is how rude I was to him when he was distressed. And now I'm distressed, just as he was back then, and I believe nothing will help me but going on a pilgrimage.'

"Now with excitement in her voice, she turned to face Mrs. Nervousness, saying, 'I was dreaming last night, and I saw Christian! Oh, how I wish my soul were with him! He lives in the presence of the King of the country and sits and eats with Him at His table. All of his companions are immortals, and the house

A CONVERSATION WITH MRS. NERVOUSNESS

that he now lives in...oh, the best palace on Earth would seem like a shack compared to it!'[1]

"She placed a hand over her chest, where her letter was securely stored. 'Not only that but the Prince of the place has sent for me with promises to receive me if I will come to Him. His messenger was just here and brought me this letter inviting me to come!' With that, she pulled out her letter and read it aloud to them. 'Now,' she said confidently, 'what do you say about this?'

"Mrs. Nervousness grunted a humorless laugh. 'Oh, the madness that has possessed both you and your husband to run headlong into difficulties. I'm sure you've heard about the troubles your husband encountered just as soon as he took his first steps away from town. Just ask your neighbor Obstinate; he'll tell you. Both he and Pliable followed along behind him on his journey until they both wised up and returned home, afraid to go any farther.

"'But even more,' she gestured, waving her hands dramatically in the air, 'we also heard how he encountered the lions, Apollyon, the Shadow of Death, and many other things. Plus, don't forget about the danger he met with at Vanity Fair. As difficult as the journey was for him, a man and all, how much more do you think it will be for a poor woman like you? And have you thought about your children—these four sweet boys, your own flesh and bone? You might be so rash as to risk your own life, but for the sake of your children, reconsider and stay at home.'

"Christiana remained sunk in thought for a brief minute then rose briskly to her feet. 'Don't tempt me, Mrs. Nervousness. I've been shown the value of this journey and everything to be gained if I'll just set out and not lose heart. I'd be the greatest fool in the world not to try. And as for all the troubles you say I'm likely to meet with along the way, that doesn't discourage me in the least bit. In fact, it just confirms that I'm right. The bitter must come before the sweet, which will make the sweet that much sweeter.'

"She then turned away from Mrs. Nervousness and continued busying herself getting ready for the journey. 'Therefore, since you didn't come to my house in God's name, as I requested, I now ask that you leave and don't bother me any further about it.'

"Mrs. Nervousness looked disdainfully at Christiana. 'Humph! Come on, Mercy. Let's leave her to her own ruin since she mocks our advice and company.'

"But Mercy didn't move. She stood there speechless, unable to answer Mrs. Nervousness for two excellent reasons.

"For one, her heart was inclined to help Christiana. After all, if her neighbor needed her and she could travel a little way on the journey to help, she would. Second, she felt the same need in her own soul that Christiana boldly said had taken hold of her mind. Mercy decided in that moment to travel with her neighbor and her sons for a short while. She owed it to herself, she thought, to see whether there was indeed truth and life in Christiana's claims. And if there was, she would commit herself and her heart to go on the journey with her.

"The morning sun beamed through the windowpanes reflecting light around the room. When Mercy finally spoke, there was a hesitancy in her voice. 'To be sure, I came with you to see Christiana this morning, and since she is, as you see, leaving the City of Destruction, I think I'll walk with her a little while on this beautiful morning to help her on her way.' However, Mercy kept her second reason to herself.

"The old woman stood brooding for a moment then shook her head and said defiantly, 'Well, it appears you're determined to be as big of a fool as she is! You should keep your wits about you, though, and be careful. While we're out of danger, we're out, but when we're in, we're in.' With that, she turned and left the house, slamming the door behind her as Christiana continued getting ready for the journey.

"Mrs. Nervousness had no sooner returned home when she called to some of her neighbors, including Mrs. Bat's-eyes, Mrs. Inconsiderate, Mrs. Light-mind, and Mrs. Know-nothing. When they arrived, she shared the story about Christiana and her intended journey.

"'As it was, ladies, I had very little to do this morning,' she said most condescendingly, 'so I went to visit Christiana. I knocked on her door like normal, and she told me to come in if I was coming in God's name. I entered, thinking all was well, until I found her preparing to leave town with her children. Well, of course I asked her what she was doing, and in short, she told me she had made up her mind and was going on a pilgrimage—just like her husband did! Oh, and yes, she also told me about a dream she had about her husband and about how the King of the country—where he is now living—had sent her a letter inviting her to come too.'

"'What!' Mrs. Know-nothing gasped in surprise. 'Do you think she'll go?'

"Mrs. Nervousness nodded. 'Oh yes, she'll go all right! There's no doubt she will leave, and I think I know why. When I tried to reason with her and persuade her to stay home because of all the trouble she's likely to encounter, she said that was one of the greatest reasons she needs to go on the journey. She told me, in so many words, that the bitter must come before the sweet, and when it does, it will only make the sweet that much sweeter.'

"'Oh, that blind and foolish woman!" said Mrs. Bat's-eyes. "Do all the trials her husband endured on his journey not warn her at all? Well, I believe if Christian were here again, he would play it safe, not putting his life in so much danger. And for what? Nothing!'

"Mrs. Inconsiderate was in no mood for such nonsense and didn't mince words. 'As far as I'm concerned, all ridiculous fools like her should leave town. Good riddance, I say! There would be no peace for any of us anyway if she stayed, especially if *that's* always on her mind. She will either be depressed, be unneighborly, or talk about things that no intelligent person can stand. I'll say it again: I'm not sorry to see her go. Let her go; then let someone better come in her place. It's never a pleasant world when these crazy fools live in it.'

"'Come, let's stop talking about this,' said Mrs. Light-mind and then abruptly changed the subject. 'Just yesterday, I was as happy as a young girl at Madam Wanton's house. And you will never guess who was there too but Mrs. Love-the-Flesh, along with Mr. Lechery, Mrs. Filth, and some others. There was music, dancing, and so much more to make you happy. And I must tell you, Mrs. Love-the-Flesh is an attractive, refined woman, and Mr. Lechery...well, let's just say he's a very handsome man.'

By this time, Christiana was on her way, and Mercy had gone along with her.

---

1. 2 Corinthians 5:1–4

Chapter Four

The Wicket Gate

"Christiana and the boys gathered their things and set out on their journey. She turned to her still very young friend with warmth in her eyes. 'Mercy, I'm so grateful that you have joined us for a while on the Way! This is completely unexpected.'

"Mercy glanced back at the city behind them. 'I would never go near the City of Destruction again if I thought it was a good idea to continue on with you.'

"Christiana's voice rose sharply as she gave way to her excitement. 'Mercy, why don't you join me and the boys? I know exactly what's at the end of our journey. My husband wouldn't trade where he is for all the gold in the Spanish mines. And since I invited you, you will not be turned away, because the King who sent for me and my children delights in offering mercy. If this all sounds good to you, I will even hire you to be our servant, understanding that there's no difference between us. Please come with us!'

"'But how can I be sure that I'll be welcomed?' she asked, shifting her stance nervously. 'If I had an assurance from someone in authority, I would go with no hesitation. At least then I'd know that He will help me when the journey becomes difficult.'

"'I have an idea,' Christiana said with a cheerful look, attempting to set the young woman's mind at ease. 'Let's go to the Wicket Gate together, and I will inquire further for you there. If you don't receive the encouragement you're searching for, I'll certainly understand if you decide to return to the City of Destruction. Also, I will even compensate you for the kindness you've shown by accompanying us to that point.'

"Mercy nodded her approval of the plan. 'Then I will go with you and see what happens. Hopefully the Lord will grant my wish, and the King of heaven will have mercy on me!'

"Christiana's heart filled with joy. Not only did she have a traveling companion but she had helped her young friend fall in love with her own salvation. But as their journey began, Mercy started crying.

"'Why are you crying?' Christiana asked curiously.

"'Oh,' she said between sobs, 'what more can I do but cry when I truthfully consider the state and condition of my poor family and the fact that they remain in that sinful town? And what makes my grief worse is that they have no one to teach them and to tell that what's to come.'

"Christiana understood this dilemma, probably as good or better than others, and told Mercy so. 'All pilgrims have a tender spot for their friends and family. My good and faithful husband, Christian, was no different. Before he left, he was in tears because I wouldn't listen to anything he had to say. However, his Lord—and ours—gathered up his tears and put them into His bottle. Now I hope the both of us, and my sweet children, are reaping the benefits of all those tears.' She lovingly placed her hand on Mercy's shoulder. 'Your tears will never be lost. Scripture tells us that those that sow with tears will reap with songs of joy. And the person who goes out weeping, carrying their precious bag of seed, will no doubt come again with rejoicing, bringing a harvest with him.'[1]

"Turning her face to heaven, Mercy prayed, 'If it's God's will to bring me to His gate, into His fold, and up His holy hill, then let the Most Blessed be my guide. And whatever comes, let Him never allow me to stray or turn away from His free grace and holy ways. Lord, I pray You will also gather the loved ones I left behind and pray that each will turn to You with all their heart and mind.'"

Now my old friend continued with his story, telling me how Christiana came to a standstill when she arrived at the Swamp of Despair. "She knew it was the place where her husband had been smothered in mud," he said, "but she also noticed that the place was worse than it was before, even though the King had commanded pilgrims to make it better."

"Is that true?" I asked, surprised.

"Yes, it's very true," said the old gentleman, shaking his head in disappointment. "There are many who pretend to be the King's workers and say they're all for fixing the King's highway. But instead of fixing it with stones, they bring dirt and manure, only making it worse. It was here that Christiana and her boys were at a standstill. It was Mercy who encouraged Christiana to go forward cautiously, carefully watching each step, and doing the best they could. More than a couple of times, Christiana felt covered in mud, but eventually they crossed over.

"Now, they had no sooner crossed over when they thought they heard someone say, 'Blessed is she who believes, because everything the Lord told her is being fulfilled.'

"Mercy glanced back at the murky swamp behind them and then forward to the gate ahead. 'If I had as much of a reason to hope for a loving reception at the Wicket Gate as you, I don't think any Swamp of Despair would ever discourage me,' she said confidently as they set out toward the gate.

"'Well, my dear Mercy,' Christiana said, slowly shaking her head and smiling as she did so, 'you know your struggles, and I know mine. I'm sure we'll encounter more than enough evil before the end of our journey. We can only imagine that people like us, who plan to attain such excellent glories as we do and are envied because of our happiness, will encounter fear, trouble, and afflictions as well as every assault by those who hate us.'"

It was at this point in my dream that Mr. Sagacity left, but I continued to dream. In this dream, I thought I saw Christiana, Mercy, and the boys all go up to the Wicket Gate, where they quickly discussed what to do and say to whomever opened the gate. Since Christiana was the oldest, they decided she should be the one to knock for entrance and speak for the rest of them to whomever opened it.

Christiana knocked, and just like her poor husband, she knocked and knocked again. But no one answered. Instead, all they heard was the sound of a large, barking dog, and it seemed to come right up on them. They were scared and didn't dare knock again for some time, all while hoping the powerful mastiff wouldn't overtake them.

Their fear soon led to confusion, and they were unsure of what to do next. They didn't dare knock because they were afraid of the dog. But they also knew if they turned and left, they would risk offending the Gate Keeper. Finally they all agreed to knock again, but this time more loudly than before.

"Who's there?" the Gate Keeper bellowed as he opened the gate, and the dog ran off to bark elsewhere.

Christiana bowed her head low. "Lord, please don't be offended by your servants for we have knocked at your princely gate."

The Keeper surveyed the group before him and spoke through resolute lips. "Where are you from, and what do you want?"

"We are from the same city as Christian and on the same mission," Christiana said rather nervously. "If you're agreeable, we would like to be admitted through this gate and then onto the Way that leads to the Celestial City. I should also mention that I'm Christiana and was the wife of Christian, who has now arrived above."

The Gate Keeper raised his eyebrows as his gaze burned through her. "What! Have you now become a pilgrim when just a short while ago you hated that life?"

She bowed her head low again, saying, "Yes, and my sweet children too."

He then took her by the hand and led her in, saying, "Let the little children come to me, and don't prevent them."[2] He then shut the gate and called to a trumpeter at the top of the gate to entertain Christiana with shouting and joyful trumpet sounds. The trumpeter obeyed and sounded his trumpet, filling the air with beautiful music.

This all happened while poor Mercy stood outside the gate trembling and crying because she feared she had been rejected.

---

1. Psalm 126:5–6
2. Matthew 19:14

Chapter Five

Intercession for Mercy

As soon as the Gate Keeper admitted Christiana and the boys through the gate, she began her appeal for Mercy. "My Lord," she said, "I have a friend standing outside the gate who's come here for the same reason as I have." She paused and glanced over at the closed gate. "I believe she's very concerned because she has arrived here without an invitation, whereas I came by invitation from my husband's King," she added by way of explanation.

Outside the gate, Mercy was becoming impatient. Each minute that passed seemed like hours. She hoped Christiana was inside pleading on her behalf, but she could stand it no longer and started knocking at the gate. She knocked so loudly it startled Christiana.

"Who's there?" the Gate Keeper asked with a look conveying He knew the answer.

When there was no reply, Christiana said anxiously, "It has to be my friend."

Opening the gate, He looked out to find Mercy unconscious on the ground. She had fainted, fearing they would never open the gate to her.

"Young lady, I command you to stand up," the Gate Keeper said, taking her by the hand.

"Oh, sir," she said, struggling to stand, "I'm so weak. I feel as though there's barely any life left in me."

"Someone once said," He replied, eyeing Mercy steadily, "'When I lost all hope, I remembered the Lord and my prayer came to you in your holy temple.'[1] Do not be afraid, Mercy, but stand up and tell me why you've come."

"I've come for the same reason as my friend Christiana, but..." she said, her voice quivering, "I didn't receive an invitation from the King as she did. My invitation was from her. I suppose that's why I'm afraid."

"Did she want you to come with her to this place?"

"Yes, she did!" Mercy recalled, adopting a more hopeful tone. "And as you can see, my Lord, I came. I'm now your servant, and if there's any grace and forgiveness that you can spare for my sins, I ask that you let me receive it."

He took Mercy again by the hand and led her gently inside the gate, saying, "I pray for all those who believe in me, by whatever means they come."[2] Turning to those standing nearby, He said, "Go get Mercy something to smell that will stop her from fainting." They returned with a bundle of myrrh that revived her.

The Lord received Christiana, her boys, and Mercy at the head of the Way and spoke kindly to them. "Lord," they said, "we're sorry for our sins and beg Your forgiveness. Please tell us what we must do next."

"I will offer you forgiveness by both word and deed—by word in the promise of forgiveness and by deed in how I obtained it. Take the first from my lips with a kiss and the other, as it will be revealed."[3]

In my dream, I saw Him telling them many good things, and they were very glad. He also brought them to the top of the gate, where He showed them the cross that saved them. Just the sight of it, he told them, would provide comfort along the Way. He then took them down to a small room built on the roof, with open windows to catch the breeze. There, He left them for a while to discuss all that had happened.

Turning to her boys and Mercy, Christiana beamed with excitement. "O Lord, how glad I am that we got in here!"

"You certainly have reason to be glad," Mercy acknowledged, collapsing into a cozy chair, "but out of all of us, I have the most cause to leap for joy!

"There was a time when I thought I had lost everything as I stood knocking at the gate and no one answered—especially when that terrible dog made such a racket barking at us!"

Mercy nodded as her smile faded. "My worst fear was being left behind after seeing you accepted by Him. I thought for sure the Scripture passage was being fulfilled that says, 'Two women will be grinding at the mill; one will be taken, and the other left.'[4] It was all I could do to keep from crying out, 'I'm done for! Ruined!' I was afraid to knock any more until I looked up and read what they wrote over the gate. I was so encouraged that I decided at the moment that I must either knock again or die, so I knocked. I do not know where the strength came from, because my spirit was struggling between life and death."

"Are you aware of how loudly you knocked at the gate?" Christiana asked, eyes wide in amazement. "Your knocks were so loud and urgent that it startled me! I'd never heard such a loud knocking in all my life. I thought for sure you would come in by force, taking the kingdom by storm."[5]

A strange, masklike expression came over the girl's face. "I was in a critical situation! What else could I have done?" she said in her own defense, her voice rising in panic. "You saw with your own eyes the door being shut on me. And, of course, there was that very cruel dog running about. Who wouldn't have knocked with all their might had they been as desperate as I was? Please tell me, what did the Lord say about my rudeness? Was He angry with me?"

With a cheerful look, Christiana attempted to set her young friend's mind at ease. "When He heard all the commotion you were making, He smiled in a most wonderful and innocent way. I actually think what you did pleased Him because He showed no sign to the contrary." She then quickly changed the subject. "But regarding the dog, I can't imagine why He keeps such an animal. Had I known about the dog before leaving, I don't know if I would have had enough courage to venture here on my own. But we're in now!" she said, looking around with a jubilant burst of laughter. "We are in! And I couldn't be happier."

Mercy didn't seem to take notice of her friend's joy but remained focused on the subject at hand. "If you think it's okay," she said with all seriousness, "the next time He comes down, I'll ask why He keeps such a filthy mongrel in His yard. I just hope He doesn't become offended."

"Yes, do!" begged the children. "And persuade Him to hang the beast because we're afraid the dog will bite us when we leave here."

When the Gate Keeper returned, Mercy fell face down and worshipped Him. "Lord," she pleaded, "please accept this offering of praise that I give to you from my own lips."

"Stand up in peace," He said to her.

But she continued face down on the ground, saying, "O Lord, you are always righteous, but I beg of you to help me understand your judgments better.[6] More specifically, I want to know why you keep such a cruel dog in your yard. Just the sight of that dog fills women and children like us with fear, and we were ready to turn and run away from the gate."

He offered an understanding nod. "That dog has another owner who lives in the castle you see over there," He replied, pointing out in the distance. "He just allows it to stay close to another man's property and, in fact, allows it to come right up to the walls of this place. Only my pilgrims can hear the great roar of his bark, which, for better or worse, has frightened many an honest pilgrim.

"There's no question that the owner doesn't have the dog for my benefit or for those pilgrims who come to see me. Instead, the intent is to make them afraid to come and knock at this gate for entrance. Sometimes the dog has even broken out and worried some that I love, but for now, I'm being patient."

He surveyed the concerned faces of His guest. "However, I help my pilgrims at just the right time," He said, seeking to reassure them, "so that they're not delivered over to the dog's power to do with them what his animalistic nature would prompt him to do."

He paused for a moment as His voice became softer but still direct. "But I can guarantee you, my dear, even had you known all this beforehand, you wouldn't have been afraid of the dog. The beggar that goes from door to door would rather run the danger of a dog bawling, barking, and biting than to lose a possible donation. And likewise, do you think that a dog's barking prevents anyone from coming to me? No!" He said emphatically. "I turn it all to the pilgrim's benefit so that I may deliver them from the mouth of lions. And my dear," He said with a faint smile twitching across his lips, "I will rescue you from the power of that dog."[7]

"I confess my ignorance," Mercy readily admitted. "I spoke about something that I didn't understand, but I know You do all things well."

Christiana then wanted to discuss their journey and get answers to some of her questions. Just as the Gate Keeper had provided for Christian, He did the same for them. He fed them, washed their feet, and instructed them how to travel along the Way.

---

1. Jonah 2:7

2. John 17:9
3. Song of Solomon 1:2, John 20:20
4. Matthew 24:41
5. Matthew 11:12
6. Jeremiah 12:1
7. Psalm 22:21–22

Chapter Six

Distracted from Danger

In my dream, they set out walking along the Way, enjoying pleasant weather as they went. Then Christiana sang, *'Bless the day that I became a pilgrim and bless the man from that place who sent me. It's true that it took me a long time to seek eternal life, but now I'm running toward it as fast as I can—and it's better late than never. All our tears will be turned to joy and our fears to faith. It's like the saying goes: How you begin often reflects how you'll end.'*

Now, there was a wall that ran like a fence along the Way on which they were traveling. On the other side of the wall was a garden belonging to the owner of the barking dog mentioned earlier. As it happened, some branches of the fruit trees growing in the garden hung over the wall, onto the Way. The fruit was ripe and pleasing to the eye, so pilgrims would find and eat the fruit, often to their own detriment.

The fruit trees fascinated Christiana's boys, and as boys tend to do, they bent the branches down and pulled off some of the fruit to eat. Their mother scolded them for doing so, but they didn't listen and continued eating the fruit.

"Well, my sons," she said, sighing in disgust, "that fruit is not ours, so what you're doing is wrong." She said this not knowing the fruit belonged to the enemy, but I'll guarantee you had she known, it would've scared her to death. But that incident passed, and they continued on their journey.

After traveling about a hundred yards from where they had entered on the Way, they spotted two men who appeared to be up to no good coming quickly down to meet them. Christiana and Mercy covered themselves with their veils and continued walking with the children, eventually arriving at the same spot on the path with the men.

The men approached the women as if to grab them, but Christiana said firmly, "You either need to stand back or go by peacefully!"

Yet the two men went on as though they didn't hear Christiana or were ignoring her and started accosting the women. Christiana became furious and began kicking them with her feet, as did Mercy, fighting them off the best they could. Christiana said to them again, "Stand back and leave us alone! We don't have any money! We are poor pilgrims, living off the charity of our friends."

"We don't want your money!" said one attacker, snickering. "There's something else we want from you. It's a small request, and if you give us what we want, we'll make women of you forever."

Christiana could only imagine what that could possibly mean. "We will neither listen to you nor give you what you ask! We're in a hurry and cannot stay. Our business is one of life or death." Once again, she and her companions made a fresh attempt to go past, but the men blocked their way.

"We intend you no harm," said the other man with feigned sincerity and a wicked smile. "It's something else that we want from you."

"There's no doubt in my mind that you want our bodies and souls. That's why you're attacking us. But we would rather die right here in this spot than allow ourselves to be led into such a trap and risk our future wellbeing."

With that, they both screamed and cried out, "Murder! Murder!" By doing so, they placed themselves under the laws that provide for the protection of women.[1] But the men continued attacking them anyway, trying to overpower them, so Christiana and Mercy cried out even louder.

As I said, they weren't more than a hundred yards from the gate where they had entered, and those in the house could hear their screams. A man by the name of Reliever, believing the screams to be those of Christiana, hurried from the house to rescue her. By the time he was in sight of the women, they were struggling with the men as the children stood by crying.

He came to their rescue, calling out to the troublemakers, saying, "What are you doing? Would you make my Lord's people sin?"

He attempted to overtake them, but they escaped over the wall into the garden of the man who owned the big dog. Once over the wall, the dog protected them. Reliever then returned to the women to see how they were doing.

"We thank your Prince!" they said, still trembling from the horrible experience. "And yes, we're fine, just somewhat frightened. We're so thankful you came to our rescue when you did; otherwise we would have surely been defeated."

Reliever listened as they told him the story of the attack. "If you knew you were weak," he said curiously, "then I'm surprised you didn't ask the Lord for a guide when you were above, visiting at the gate. Had you done so, and He provided you one, you probably would have avoided troubles and dangers just like this."

Christiana shook her head, obviously disappointed in herself. "Unfortunately, we were so consumed with the blessing we received that we completely forgot about any dangers that we might encounter along the Way. Besides, who could have imagined such wicked men would lurk about so near the King's palace? Yes, there's no question. We should have asked the Lord for a guide." She paused for a moment and then added, "I'm curious though. Why didn't He offer to send one along with us from the start? Surely He would've known a guide would've helped us."

"It's not always necessary to give things that are not asked for," said Reliever. "By doing so, those things become of little value. But when you want something bad enough that you can feel it—the preciousness of it—that's when what's given will be used. Had my Lord given you a guide without your asking for one, would you have regretted your oversight as you do now? No! So all things—like forgetting to ask for a guide—work for good because now you'll be more aware."

Christiana glanced back at the gate behind them. "Should we return to my Lord once again to confess our mistake and ask for one?"

"I will present Him with your confession of your mistake," he said, shaking his head decisively. "You don't need to go back again, because in all the places where you're going, you'll find no lack of help. In every one of my Lord's lodgings that He has prepared for the care of His pilgrims, there's enough to provide them with help against all such attempts as the one you just experienced. But as I said, the pilgrims will ask Him to do it for them. And it's a poor thing that's not worth asking for."[2] After saying this, he returned to his place, and the pilgrims went on their way.

"Suddenly I feel very confused!" said Mercy, her gaze fixed upon Christiana. "I thought we were past all danger and would never see such pain and suffering again."

Christiana nodded without looking at her. "My sister, your innocence may offer you a good excuse, but as for me, my fault is so much greater. I saw the danger before stepping out of the door of my home, yet I made no plans to provide for myself when I could have. I'm afraid that I bear much of the blame."

Confusion spread across the young woman's face. "How could you possibly have known any of this before leaving your home? Please explain this mystery to me."

Christiana then recounted the dream she had while lying in bed one night after a day of being very troubled about her own salvation. "Before I set one foot out of town, I saw two men in my dream, much like the two who attacked us, standing at the foot of my bed. They were plotting how best to prevent my salvation, and I'll tell you exactly what they said. They said, 'What should we do with this woman? She cries out when she's awake and asleep for forgiveness. If she's allowed to go on like this, we'll lose her just like we lost her husband.' As you can see, this should've warned me to provide for myself when provisions were available."

Mercy considered this and said understandingly, "Well, because of your negligence, we're aware of our own imperfections now. The Lord used this opportunity to make known the riches of His grace. He followed us with kindness that we didn't ask for and delivered us for His good pleasure from the hands of those men who were stronger than us."

---

1. Deuteronomy 22:25–27
2. Ezekiel 36:37

Chapter Seven

The Interpreter's House

They continued talking on their journey until they arrived at the Interpreter's house, which stood along the Way. You'll find more detailed information about this house, which was built as a place for pilgrims to find rest, in the first story of the Pilgrim's Progress.

As they approached the door, they overheard some pleasant conversation happening inside the house. More specifically, they thought they heard Christiana's name mentioned in the discussion. By this time, the news about her and the boys leaving the City of Destruction to go on a pilgrimage had already reached those in the house. They were glad to hear this news because they knew she was Christian's wife—the same woman who some time ago had refused to listen to anything about going on a pilgrimage.

However, those inside the house didn't know Christiana and Mercy were standing quietly at the door, listening to all the good things being said about her. After some time, Christiana knocked at the door, just like she had at the gate earlier.

A young woman named Innocent answered the door. She surveyed the two women before her then asked pleasantly, "Who would you like to speak with here?"

"We understand this place has been prepared for those who have become pilgrims," said Christiana. "We are now pilgrims and have come hoping to receive all that has been prepared for us. As you can see, the day is almost over, and we're reluctant to go any further into the night."

Innocent nodded and smiled. "Please tell me your names so that I may tell my lord inside."

"My name is Christiana. I was the wife of the pilgrim who traveled through here some years ago, and these are his four children. This young woman traveling with me is going on a pilgrimage too."

Leaving them at the door, Innocent ran to tell those inside the house. "You won't believe who's at the door! It's Christiana, her children, and a companion all waiting to be admitted." They leaped for joy and went and told their master, whose name was the Interpreter.

The Interpreter came to the door and asked, "Are you Christiana, the wife whom Christian the good man left behind when he devoted himself to the pilgrim's life?"

The smile that had been on Christiana's face since arriving faded as she recalled her painful past. "Yes, I'm that woman who was so hardhearted that I neglected my husband's troubles. I then let him leave to travel his journey alone. These are his four children. But now I've come because I'm also convinced this is the only right way."

The Interpreter clasped his hands together happily. "Then Scripture has been fulfilled as in the man's story who said to his son, 'Go, work today in my vineyard; and he said to his father, I will not; but afterwards he repented and went.'"[1]

THE INTERPRETER'S HOUSE   35

"Amen!" Christiana exclaimed. "This is true of my own life when at last I was granted peace with Him, without spot and blameless!"

"But why are you standing at the door?" he asked, waving them in. "Come in, you blessed one! We were just talking about you, and now you've come to us for advice about how to journey as a pilgrim. Come, children, come in!" he said, motioning to the boys and Mercy. "Come, young woman, come in!"

Once inside, they were all encouraged to sit down and rest awhile. Those who ministered to the pilgrims in the house came into the room and smiled after seeing them, overjoyed that Christiana was now a pilgrim. They looked after the boys, tenderly caressing their faces as a kind gesture of receiving them. They also lovingly cared for Mercy and welcomed all of them into their master's house.

Since supper was not ready yet, the Interpreter took them to visit his most important rooms in the house. He showed them what Christian, Christiana's husband, had seen some time before. It was here that they saw the man in the cage, the man and his dream, the man who cut his way through his enemies, and the picture of the biggest of them all. He showed them everything that was so beneficial to Christian when he was there.

Christiana and those with her spent some time thinking about all they had seen. Then the Interpreter took them aside once again to visit more rooms. He led them first into a room where there was a man who could only look down and was holding a muckrake. Standing above him was a man holding a celestial crown, offering to give the man the crown for the muckrake. However, the man refused to look up nor would he listen to the man with the crown. Instead, he just continued to rake to himself the straws, small sticks, and dust on the floor.

"I think I somewhat understand the meaning of this," Christiana said, studying the scene. "This represents worldly man...does it not, good sir?"

"You're correct," he said, smiling approvingly. "The muckrake illustrates the man's worldly mind. As you can see, this man is more interested in raking up the straws, sticks, and dust on the floor rather than accepting the celestial crown being offered to him. From this we understand that for some people, heaven is nothing more than a fable, while the things of this earth are of the utmost importance. But there's more too, in that the man with the rake can only look downward. When earthly things hold power over the minds of men, they will completely carry their hearts away from God."

"Oh, deliver me from this muckrake!" Christiana said, quick to respond.[2]

The Interpreter frowned and shook his head as he answered, "That prayer is so overused that it's almost rusty. 'Don't make me rich' is seldom prayed by one in ten thousand people today. With most, straws, sticks, and dust are the great things they now search for."

Both Mercy and Christiana wept. "Oh, it's too true!"

He then took them to the very best room in the house; a very grand room it was. He told them to look all around to see if they could find anything. They looked all around, but there was nothing to be seen in the room except an enormous spider on the wall—which they intentionally overlooked.

Mercy said, "Sir, I see nothing." But Christiana didn't say a word.

The Interpreter raised his eyebrows and made a slight gesture back to the room. "Look again."

Mercy looked again and this time said, "I see nothing here but an ugly spider hanging by her hands on the wall."

"Is there only one spider in *all* this spacious room?" he asked, emphasizing the word *all*.

Tears welled up in Christiana's eyes because she was a quick learner. "Yes, my lord," she said, "there's more than one spider here whose venom is far more destructive than hers."

The Interpreter looked pleased. "You're telling the truth."

This made Mercy blush, and the boys covered their faces because they all understood the riddle now.

"You can take hold of a spider with your hands," he said, "but as you can see, it's still found in royal palaces.[3] The reason this is recorded is to show you that regardless of how full of the venom of sin you may be, you can, by the hand of faith, lay hold of and live in the best room that belongs to the King's house above."

"I thought it was something like this," Christiana said, studying the scene attentively, "but couldn't figure it all out. I thought we were like spiders—ugly creatures that could be found in no matter how fine a room. But it never occurred to me that this spider, this venomous and ugly creature, represents our learning how to act in faith. And yet, since this spider has taken hold of and lives in the best room in the house, I can see that God has made nothing in vain."

They were all happy, looking at each other with tears in their eyes, then bowed before the Interpreter.

He then took them into another room, where there was a hen and chickens, and told them to observe for a while. One chicken went to the trough to drink, and every time she drank, she lifted her head and eyes toward heaven.

He motioned toward the chicken. "Do you see what this little chick is doing? Learn from it so that you will always acknowledge where your mercies come from—receiving them with your eyes looking to heaven." He then pointed back to the animals. "But there's more. Observe and watch again."

They all paid attention and watched the hen communicate with her chicks in four different ways. First, she had a common call that she used all day long. Second, she had a special call that she used only occasionally. Third, she made a caring sound, and finally, she had an outcry.[4]

"Now," he said, turning his attention back to his guests, "compare this hen to your King and these chicks to his obedient servants. For just as the chicks are answerable to the hen, He Himself has methods by which He communicates with His people. By His common call, He gives nothing, and by His special call, He always has something to give. He also has a caring voice for those that are under His wing and an outcry to warn us when He sees the enemy coming. My darlings, I led you into this room to show you these things because as women, you can more easily understand."

Christiana was eager to see everything she could. "Sir, please show us more."

The Interpreter agreed and led them into the slaughterhouse where the butcher was killing a sheep, and as they watched, the sheep was quiet and accepted her death patiently.

"You must learn from this sheep to suffer and to put up with wrongs without grumbling and complaining," he said. "Look how quietly she accepts her death—and without objecting. She allows her skin to be pulled over her ears. Your King calls you His sheep."

After this, he led them into his garden, where there was a great variety of flowers. "Do you see all these flowers?" he asked.

"Yes," Christiana responded.

"Pay close attention to the flowers. They are all different sizes, quality, color, smell, and strength, and some are better than others. Also, they stand where the gardener has planted them, not quarreling with one another."

Again he led them into his field, which he had sowed with wheat and corn. But when they looked at the crops, they noticed the tops were all cut off and only the straw remained.

"This ground was fertilized, plowed, and sowed, but what should we do with the crop?" he asked, casting an appraising gaze across the group.

Christiana felt sure she knew this answer. "Burn some and make fertilizer of the rest."

"You're looking for fruit, and if you do not find it, you send it to the fire to be trampled under men's feet," he replied. He paused and then said more thoughtfully, "However, be careful when making this judgment that you don't also condemn yourselves."

As they were coming back from the field, they spotted a little robin with a great spider in his mouth. "Look here," the Interpreter said, pointing at the robin.

Mercy wondered what they were looking at, but Christiana said, "What a disgrace to see such a pretty little bird like the red-breasted robin acting is this manner. Many consider this bird to be their favorite because they're so lovely to have around! I thought they lived on crumbs of bread or on other such harmless matter. I don't like that bird anymore."

"This robin is an excellent example to describe some people who profess Christ," he said. "To look at them, they appear like this robin—notably pretty because of their color and behavior—and they seem to have a very great love for those that are true believers. But more than that, they also show a desire to associate with these believers and to be in their company—as if they could live on the crumbs of good men. It is for this reason that they pretend when visiting the house of a godly person or when doing the Lord's work. But when alone, like this robin, they can catch and gobble up spiders. They can change their diet, drink wickedness, and swallow down sin like water."

When they arrived back at the house, they found that supper was still not ready. Christiana turned to the Interpreter and asked if there was anything else he could show or explain to them that would be beneficial for their journey.

For a moment, the Interpreter thought, then said, "The fatter the sow is, the more she desires the mud. The fatter the ox is, the more thoughtlessly he goes to the slaughter, and the healthier a lustful man is, the more prone he is to do evil. There's a desire for women to look beautiful, and it's a beautiful thing to be adorned with that which is valuable in God's sight. It's easier to keep watch for a night or two than to sit up for an entire year together. In the same way, it's easier to be faithful in the beginning than to hold out to the end as we should.

"When encountering a storm, every shipmaster will willingly cast overboard anything of the smallest value in the vessel, but who throws the best out first? No one—except those that don't fear God. One leak will sink a ship, and one sin will destroy a sinner.

"When you forget your friends, you're ungrateful to them, but when you forget your Savior, you're unmerciful to yourself. The one who lives in sin and looks for happiness afterward is like the one who sows weeds and hopes to fill his barn with wheat or barley. If you want to live a good life, keep in mind your very last day; then live accordingly. Gossiping and distracting thoughts prove that sin is in the world. If the world, for which God provided light, is valuable to men, how much more should we value heaven, for which God gives praise! If we're unwilling to let a life filled with so many troubles pass us by, what will life be like above? Everybody is so willing to praise the goodness of men, but who is affected by the goodness of God as he should be? We seldom sit down for a meal, but we eat and leave. In the same way, there's more virtue and righteousness in Jesus Christ than the entire world has need of."

When the Interpreter was done, he took them out into his garden again and led them to a tree. The insides were all rotten and gone, and yet it grew and had leaves.

"What does this mean?" Mercy asked him.

THE INTERPRETER'S HOUSE

"This tree," he said, "whose outside is pretty and whose inside is rotten, is like many who are in the garden of God. They speak highly on God's behalf but will do nothing for Him. Their leaves are pretty, but their hearts are not good for anything except firewood for the devil's tinderbox."

By this time, supper was ready, and they spread a variety of food out on the sideboard. After giving thanks, they sat down and ate.

---

1. Matthew 21:29
2. Proverbs 30:8
3. Proverbs 30:28
4. Matthew 23:37

Chapter Eight

Great Heart Leads the Women

The Interpreter entertained the pilgrims at the meal with music, as was customary for any who visited. The minstrels played, and there was one with a magnificent voice who sang, "The Lord is my only support and the only One who feeds me. How can I then be in want or need of anything?"

When the song and music ended, the Interpreter asked Christiana what it was that first motivated her to become a pilgrim.

She thought for a moment, once again pulling from her painful past. "Well, initially my mind was overcome with genuine grief after losing my husband. But I also thought about all of Christian's struggles before he began his own pilgrimage, not to mention how unkind I had been toward him. This consumed me with so much guilt that I could've drowned myself in a pond."

Her eyes then brightened. "But it was in that very moment that I had a dream. It was about how happy and well Christian was where he was living. Then I received a letter from the King of that country inviting me to come. The dream combined with the letter weighed so heavily on my mind that it compelled me to go on this journey."

He raised a brow inquisitively. "Did you meet with any opposition before leaving home?"

"Yes, one...a neighbor of mine, Mrs. Nervousness. She was related to the man who tried to persuade my husband to return home for fear of the lions. In much the same way, she all but called me a fool for heading out on such a desperate adventure, as she called it. She did all she could to discourage me, which included reminding me of all the hardships and troubles that Christian encountered—all of which I handled fairly well."

Christiana made a grimace. "But what has troubled me most is a dream I had about two wicked men who were plotting how to make me fail on my journey. Those thoughts still consume me, making me fearful of everyone I meet in case they might try to hurt me or get me off my path."

She glanced over at Mercy then back to the Interpreter. "I'll tell you, my lord, but I wouldn't want everyone to know," she said hesitantly, her voice now softer, "that both Mercy and I were severely attacked on the Way between leaving the gate and arriving at this house. It was so bad that we cried out 'Murder!' And the two men who attacked us were just like the two I saw in my dream."

"Your beginning was good, and as you get close to your final ending, it will be so much better," he said encouragingly before turning his attention to Mercy. "And what motivated you to come here, sweetheart?"

Mercy blushed and trembled but remained quiet for a while.

His eyes were soft and comforting. "Don't be afraid. Just believe and speak your mind."

"Truly, sir," she began, her voice quivering, "my lack of knowledge is why I wish to be silent and is what also fills me with a fear of coming up short in the end. Unlike my friend Christiana, I can't tell you of any visions or dreams that I've had. I also don't know what it's like to mourn over refusing the good advice of family."

"What was it then, dear heart, that encouraged you to do as you have done?" he asked.

Mercy shifted in her seat uncomfortably. "Well, it just so happened that when Christiana was packing up to leave the City of Destruction, I and another went to see her and knocked at her door. When we went inside and saw her preparing to leave, we asked her what she was doing. She told us she had received an invitation to join her husband. Then she told us how she had seen him in a dream, living in a wonderful place among immortals, wearing a crown, playing a harp, eating, and drinking at his Prince's table and singing praises to Him for bringing him there and so on.

"Now, while she was telling us these things, I felt my heart burning inside me. I said to myself, 'If this is true, I'll leave my father and my mother and the land of my birth and go along with Christiana if I can.' So I asked her to explain the truth of these matters and if she would allow me to go with her. It was obvious that the only thing remaining in our town for me was danger and ruin. I left with a heavy heart—not because I was unwilling to leave but because I was leaving so much family behind. However, I've come with all the desire of my heart and will go, if I can, with Christiana to her husband and his King."

The Interpreter nodded approvingly. "Leaving the City of Destruction was good and the right thing to do. You're like Ruth, who left her father and mother because she loved Naomi and the Lord her God. She left the land of her birth to go live with people that she did not know beforehand. May the Lord bless your work, and may you be given a full reward from the Lord God of Israel, under whose wings you have come to trust."[1]

Once supper ended and preparation was made for bed, the women each went to their own rooms and the boys together in another room. But Mercy couldn't sleep. She lay in bed, overjoyed that all the lingering doubts she had been harboring were now removed and she blessed and praised God, who had been so good to her.

In the morning, they got up with the sun and prepared to leave, but the Interpreter wanted them to stay around for a while because he wanted them to leave in a proper manner. He then instructed Innocent to take them into the garden to bathe them, cleaning off any dirt they had collected while traveling.

Innocent took them to the bath in the garden and told them they must wash and get clean. It was her master's request that all women who arrived at the house bathe before continuing their pilgrimage. They all went in the bath and washed, including the boys, and came out not only sweet and clean but also full of energy, strengthened in their joints. They looked and felt so much better than before they had bathed.

When they had returned from bathing in the garden, the Interpreter gathered them together to look at them. "As lovely as the moon!" he said with a smile.

Then he called for the seal that was used to seal those who had been bathed. The seal was brought, and the Interpreter placed his mark on them so they would be known in the places where they were yet to go. Now the seal was the sum and substance of the Passover, which the children of Israel ate when they came out of the land of Egypt.[2] The mark was placed between their eyes, greatly adding to their beauty because it embellished their faces. It also added to their glory and made their appearance more like that of angels.

The Interpreter spoke to the young woman who was waiting on these women. "Go into the sacred room, and bring out some clothes for these people."

She left and returned with white clothes and laid them down before him. It was fine linen, white and clean, and he instructed them to dress. Once dressed, the women seemed to be afraid of each other because neither could see the glory in themselves but they could see the glory in each other. Because of this, they now regarded each other more highly than themselves.

"You're more beautiful than I," they each told the other. The children also stood amazed to see their new appearance.

The Interpreter then called for one of his male servants by the name of Great Heart and told him to get his sword, helmet, and shield. "Take these women...my daughters," he said tenderly, "and accompany them to the house called Beautiful, which is where they will rest next." So Great Heart took his weapons and went before them.

"Godspeed!" the Interpreter called out to them as they were leaving. Those who belonged to the family also came out and wished them farewell.

They went on their way singing, "This place has been our second stop. It was here that we heard and saw good things that, from age to age, have been hidden from others. The raker, spider, the hen, the chicken too, have taught us a lesson. Let us now learn from it.

"The butcher, garden, and the field, the robin, and his bait, also the rotten tree yields for me an argument of weight that moves me to watch and pray, to strive to be sincere, to take my cross up day by day, and serve the Lord with fear."

---

1. Ruth 2:11–12
2. Exodus 13:8–10

Chapter Nine

The Consequences of the Cross

In my dream, I saw Great Heart leading them along the Way, eventually arriving at the place where Christian's burden fell off his back and rolled into a tomb. It was here they stopped to praise God.

The sight reminded Christiana of what they were told at the gate about receiving forgiveness by both word and deed—by word in the promise of forgiveness and by deed in how forgiveness was accomplished. "I know something of what the promise of forgiveness is," she said, recalling the event to the others, "but what does it mean to receive it by deed, and how exactly was the deed accomplished? Mr. Great Heart, I suppose you know the answer, and we would appreciate your sharing your thoughts on the matter."

Great Heart turned to face the group and spoke through resolute lips. "Forgiveness by deed is when someone acquires forgiveness for another person who needs it and who cannot obtain it on their own. This is how I got it. So to answer your broader question, another person acquired the forgiveness that you, Mercy, and these boys received, namely, He who let you in at the gate. And how did He get it? He did so in two ways.

First He provided righteousness to cover you and then spilled His blood to wash you."

Christiana wrinkled her forehead. "But if He parts with His righteousness by giving it to us, what will He have for Himself?"

Their fearless guide let out a great laugh. "He has more righteousness than you could possibly need or that He needs Himself."

She smiled faintly, as if to say that she still didn't understand. "Can you please explain that a little better?"

He met her gaze and saw the confusion that crossed her features. "I would be glad to, but first I must tell you that the one whom we are to speak of is like no other. He has two natures in one—a godly nature and a human nature. They're clearly seen as different but impossible to divide. Each nature has its own righteousness that's essential to that nature. However, if either nature's righteousness were to be removed, it would cause that nature to die. We don't have this righteousness, but He can place it upon us to make us righteous and live accordingly.

"In addition, He also has another righteousness that's different from the other two because it serves to create a union between both natures. This is essential to His fulfilling the role of mediator between God and man—a role which has been prepared for and entrusted to Him."

Great Heart continued to elaborate as his audience listened attentively. "Now, if He were to part with His godly righteousness, He would cease to be God. And if He were to part with His human righteousness, His humanity would no longer be pure. But if He were to part with the third, well...He would then cast aside that perfection that allows Him to fulfill the role of mediator. You see, this third righteousness comes by deed and obedience to God's revealed will. It's what He places upon sinners to cover their sins and why it says, 'For as by the one man's disobedience the many were made sinners, so by the one man's obedience the many will be made righteous.'"[1]

She was starting to understand, but some lingering questions remained. "So does this mean that the other two types of righteousness are of no use to us?"

"Oh yes," he said, nodding, "the first two are essential to His nature and purpose, but they cannot be passed on to another. The power of the first two gives authority to the third—the one that offers forgiveness and makes His righteousness so effective. And so the righteousness of His godly nature gives Him power to be obedient, whereas the righteousness of His human nature makes it possible for His obedience to forgive. As a result, the righteousness that joins these two natures now has the authority to do the work for which it was ordained.

"Now, there's this first righteousness that Christ, as God, has no need of because without it, He is God. Then there's a second righteousness that Christ, as man, has no need of because He is a perfect man without it. And then there is this third righteousness that Christ, as God and man, has no need of because He's God without it and therefore He can spare it. It's a justifying righteousness that He doesn't want for Himself and freely gives away. For this reason, it's called the gift of righteousness."[2]

Great Heart let his words sink in a moment. It was a lot for them to consider but nevertheless important. He began again, this time speaking a little more slowly. "Now, since Christ Jesus our Lord has made Himself under the law, this righteousness must be given away. Why? Because the law binds those under it to do right by their neighbor and to do so in love. And according to the law, if a man has two coats, he should give one to another who is in need. If we were to expand this analogy, the Lord then has two coats: one for Himself and one to spare. Therefore, He freely gives one to those that have none. And in the same way, Christiana and Mercy, and the rest of you, your forgiveness came by deed...or, in other words, by the work of another man. Your Lord Christ is the one who worked and then gives away what He worked for to the next poor beggar he meets."

Great Heart raised a finger as if to emphasize his next point. "But in order to provide forgiveness by deed, there must be a price paid to God and something prepared to cover us with as well. Sin has delivered us over to the just curse of a righteous law. As a result, we must now be justified from this curse by being redeemed or, more specifically, having a price paid for the harms we have done. The Lord accomplished this through His blood by standing in your place and dying your death for your sins. In this way, He ransomed you from your sins by blood and covered your polluted and deformed souls with His righteousness.[3] Because of this, God passes you over and will not hurt you when he comes to judge the world."[4]

The gleam in Christiana's eyes grew brighter. "This is amazing! Now I understand what it means to be forgiven by word and deed. Mercy, my good friend, let's work together to remember this, and my children, you would do well to remember it too." She paused for a moment then added, "Sir, is this what made my dear husband's burden fall from off his shoulders, causing him to leap for joy?"

Great Heart nodded. "Yes, it was. Christian's belief in this very thing cut those strings from his burden that couldn't be cut by other means, and it provided him the truth to why he had suffered carrying his burden to the cross."

"I thought so," she said, smiling, "because even though my heart was full of light and joy before, it's ten times brighter and more joyful now. And even though these feelings are new to me, I'm now convinced that if the most burdened man in the world were here and saw and believed as I do now, his heart would be as joyful and happy as mine."

"Redemption offers comfort and eases your burden," he assured her, returning a smile, "but it also creates a love inside our hearts. If a redeemed person truly believes not just in the promise of forgiveness but that the deed of one man accomplished it for them, how could it not affect them? How could they not love that man who made it possible for them?"

"So true," she said. "It's as if my heart bleeds when I think of Him bleeding for me. It cries out, 'You're loving and blessed, and You deserve to have all of me because You bought me! You paid a price for me that's ten thousand times more than I'm worth.' Why then should I be surprised that this brought tears to my husband's eyes and encouraged him to march so swiftly along? I'm convinced that he wanted me to join him, but I was such a vile wretch! I let him come all alone. Oh, Mercy, if only your father and mother were here and Mrs. Nervousness too! But not just them. I also wish with all my heart that Madam Wanton was here too. Surely, surely, their hearts would be affected and not pulled away to return home out of fear or lust. If so, they would miss their chance to become good pilgrims."

"You're speaking with kindness and love now, but do you think you'll always feel this way?" he asked with a questioning gaze. "The fact is, not everyone does, not even those who saw the blood of Jesus. There were some who stood by, watching blood run from His heart to the ground, and were not affected by it at all. Instead of weeping, they laughed at Him. Instead of becoming His disciples, they hardened their hearts against Him. All that you have, my daughters, everything that I've told you about, you have by a personal impression made possible by a divine purpose. Remember what was told to you earlier about the hen and how her common call gave no food to her chicks? Therefore, this is known to you by a special grace."

---

1. Romans 5:19
2. Romans 5:17
3. Romans 8:34
4. Galatians 3:13

Chapter Ten

Following the Path of Christian

Now I saw in my dream that they continued their journey until arriving at the same place where Simple, Lazy, and Arrogance had lain asleep when Christian passed through on his pilgrimage. They found the three men hanging up in irons a little off on the other side of the Way.

Mercy turned to their guide, asking curiously, "Who are these three men, and why are they hung here?"

"These three are men of poor character. They have no interest in becoming pilgrims, and whoever else they can try to stop from becoming one, they do so. They are lazy and foolish themselves and try to persuade others to do the same, saying that all will be well in the end. They were asleep when Christian passed by here, and now, as you pass, they have been hanged."

"Were they able to persuade others to their opinion?" Mercy asked him.

"Yes, they turned several off the Way," he said. "There was Slow-pace, whom they convinced to become just like them. But there were others too, including Short-wind, No-heart, Linger-after-lust, Sleepy-head, and a young woman named Dull, all of whom they successfully turned off the Way to become like them. They would persuade others by telling bad information about your Lord, specifically that He was a slave driver. They also spread an evil report about the Good Land, saying it was not half as good as some pretended it to be. Then they would tell lies about His servants, considering even the very best of them meddlesome, troublesome busybodies. Also, they would call the bread of God trash, the comforts of His children imaginary, and the missionary work of pilgrims pointless and of no purpose."

"No!" said Christiana, her voice sounding incredulous. "If this is how they were, I will never cry over them. As far as I'm concerned, they're getting what they deserve being hung by the highway to warn others. But wouldn't it have been better had they engraved their crimes and misdemeanors on some iron or brass plate to warn other wicked men?"

Great Heart pointed over at the men. "You will see it's already there if you go a little closer to the wall."

"No, no," Mercy quickly retorted, perfectly fine to keep her distance. "Let them hang and their names rot while their crimes live forever against them. I think someone did us a favor by hanging them before we arrived. Who knows what they might have done to such poor women as us?"

Then she turned it into a song, singing, "Now then, you three, hang there, and be a sign to all that come against the truth; And let him who comes after fear this end, if unto pilgrims he is not a friend; And you, my soul, beware of all such men like these, who oppose holiness."

They continued on the Way until they came to the bottom of the Hill of Difficulty, where once again their good friend Great Heart took the opportunity to share what had happened when Christian passed through there.

First, he took them to the spring. "Look," he said. "This is the spring Christian drank from before going up this hill. Then it was clear and good, but now it's muddy and trampled through by some who don't want pilgrims to quench their thirst."[1]

"I wonder why they're so spiteful." Mercy said.

Their guide shrugged and shook his head without answering her directly. "The water will be fine if you first draw it into a container that's sweet and good, allowing the dirt to sink to the bottom. Then the water will come out clear."

So that's what Christiana and her companions did. They filled up a clay pot with some water and let it stand until the dirt fell to the bottom before drinking it.

Next he showed them the intersection of two roads at the bottom of the hill where Formalism and Hypocrisy got lost. "These are dangerous paths." His voice was stern with warning. "In fact, two men lost their way on these paths when Christian came through here. Now you can see that both roads have since been blocked with chains, posts, and a ditch, but there are still some that choose to take a chance here rather than take the more difficult path up the hill."

"The way of transgressors is hard," said Christiana, surveying all the obstacles. "It's a wonder how anyone ventures into those paths without the risk of breaking their neck."[2]

"I agree," said Great Heart, "but they do it all the time. And when any of the King's servants see them, they call out, warning them they are on the wrong path and of the danger ahead. But they just answer disparagingly, saying, 'We will not listen to the words you have told us in the King's name, but we will certainly do whatever we want and decide to on our own.'[3] And if you look a little closer, you'll see that there is ample warning, not only by the chain, posts, and ditch but there's also a border around it. But even with all these warnings, there are still some that choose to go there."

Christiana frowned, shaking her head. "They're lazy and don't love hard work or the effort it takes to go up the hill. It seems unpleasant to them. They're perfect examples of what's written about the way of the lazy man being a hedge of thorns. For whatever reason, they choose to walk straight into a trap rather than go up this hill and the rest of the way to the Celestial City."[4]

Then they went forward and walked up the hill. But before reaching the top, Christiana was breathing hard. "I dare say this is a tough hill! I'm not surprised by those that choose a smoother path because they love the easy life more than their own souls."

"I must sit down," Mercy said, looking for a place to rest just as the youngest child began to cry.

"Come, come," said Great Heart, motioning for them to keep moving, "don't sit down here, because the Prince's arbor is just a little bit farther." He then took the little boy by the hand and led him up to it.

They were sweltering hot by the time they reached the arbor and couldn't wait to sit down. "Rest is so sweet to those who work hard," said Mercy, collapsing onto a bench inside the arbor. "The Prince is so good at providing resting places for His pilgrims! I've heard a lot about this arbor but never seen it. However, what I heard is that we should beware of falling asleep because it cost poor Christian."

Great Heart was smiling. "Come over here, boys," he said, inviting the boys to join him where he sat. "How are you, and what do you think about going on a pilgrimage now?"

The youngest boy, named James, spoke up. "Sir, thank you for lending me a hand when I needed it most. I was almost ready to give up. I'm reminded of what my mother always told me—that the way to heaven is up a ladder and the way to hell is as down a hill. Personally, I'd rather go up the ladder to life than down the hill to death."

Mercy tilted her head awkwardly. "But the proverb says to go downhill is easy."

The young man was unmovable in his determination. "In my opinion, the day is coming when going downhill will be the hardest of all."

"That's a good boy," said his master with a great, hearty laugh. "You have given her the right answer." Mercy smiled, and the little boy blushed.

"Come," said Christiana, reaching into her bag, "we need to eat a little to curb our appetite while sitting here resting our legs. I have some fruit that Mr. Interpreter gave me just as I was walking out his door. He also gave me some honeycomb and a little bottle of reviving spirits."

Mercy gave her old friend a side glance. "I thought he gave you something because I saw him call you aside."

"Yes, he did," said Christiana, passing out the food, "but, Mercy, what I said before leaving home still stands—that you will share in all the good that comes my way because you so willingly came along as my friend." Then she gave food to both Mercy and the boys, and they ate. She turned to offer some to Great Heart. "Sir, will you join us in eating something?"

He shook his head. "You're traveling on a pilgrimage, and this food is doing you much good. I'll be returning home soon and can eat that same food every day." So they ate, drank, and chatted for a while as the evening started setting in.

---

1. Ezekiel 34:18–19
2. Proverbs 13:15
3. Jeremiah 44:16–17
4. Proverbs 15:19

Chapter Eleven

An Encounter with Grim

Great Heart stood and addressed the others. "It's getting late. Perhaps it's best if we prepare to leave."

They got up to go as the boys led the way, but Christiana forgot to take her bottle of reviving spirits, so she sent James back to fetch it.

Mercy shook her head slowly. "I think this is a place for losing things. Christian lost his certificate here, and Christiana left her bottle behind. Sir, what causes this?" she asked, looking slightly bewildered.

"The cause is sleep or forgetfulness," he said. "Some sleep when they should stay awake, and some forget when they should remember. This is often the very reason some pilgrims end up losing things at resting places. Pilgrims should be careful and remember what they've already received, even in their greatest moments. When we forget to do so, our rejoicing often ends in tears and our sunny days turn cloudy—like what happened to Christian when he visited this place."

When they arrived at the place where Mistrust and Nervousness had met Christian to persuade him to turn back for fear of the lions, they saw something that looked like a stage. Directly in front of it, facing the road, was a broad plate with a verse written on it. There was also writing below the plate explaining the reason for the construction of the stage. The verse read, "Let the one who sees this stage be careful what they think and say in order to avoid moving along too quickly, as some have done in the past."

The words below the verse read, "This stage is here to punish those who, because of nervousness and lack of faith, are afraid to go any farther on their pilgrimage. On this stage, Mistrust and Nervousness were both burned through the tongue with a hot iron for trying to delay Christian on his journey."

Mercy read and then reread the verse closely. "This is just like the saying of the Beloved: 'You deceitful tongue, what can the Lord give you? What more can he do for you? He will give you a warrior's sharpened arrows and red-hot coals.'"[1]

They continued until they came within sight of the lions. Now, Great Heart was a strong man and not afraid of the lions, but when they came up to the place where the lions were, the boys, who had been leading the way, became scared and fell back behind the others because they were afraid of the lions.

"Tell me now, my boys," their guide said, smiling, "why is it you love leading the way when there's no danger approaching but then love to run behind us as soon as the lions appear?"

As they approached the lions, Great Heart drew his sword, intending to make a way for the pilgrims to pass despite the beasts.

Suddenly, a giant of a man appeared before them, who seemed to be the master of the lions. His name was Grim, or Bloody-man, because he had killed many pilgrims. "What's your reason for coming here?" he roared to the pilgrims' guide.

Great Heart gripped his sword tightly. "These women and children are on a pilgrimage, and this is the way they must go. And they will go this way, undeterred by you or these lions."

Grim didn't move. "This is not their way, and they will not enter! I'm here to stop them and will back the lions."

To tell the truth, the ferociousness of the roaring lions and the foreboding presence of Grim had left this path unoccupied for some time and grass had overgrown most of it.

Christiana hesitantly, but boldly took a stand. "Though these highways have been abandoned until now and even though travelers have wasted time taking back roads, it will not be so today! I'm a risen mother in Israel!"[2]

Ignoring her, Grim swore they would not pass and stood firmly by his lions, warning his unwanted guests to turn away. But Great Heart, the pilgrims' brave guide, made his approach toward Grim, striking him so hard with his sword that he forced the giant to retreat.

"Will you kill me on my own ground?" Grim said, staggering around with sudden realization of his imminent defeat.

"This is not your ground!" Great Heart adamantly declared. "This is the King's highway we're on, and you've placed your lions on it. These women and children are weak, but they will pass through despite your lions."

And with that, he struck the giant down hard, bringing him to his knees and breaking his helmet. With the next blow, he cut off one of his adversary's arms. The giant's roar was so hideous that it frightened the women, and yet at the same time, they were glad to see him lying sprawled on the ground.

The chained lions could do nothing to help, while old Grim, who intended to back them, fell dead. Great Heart turned to the pilgrims. "Come now and follow me, and the lions will not hurt you." The women did as they were told but shook with fear as they passed by the lions. The boys thought they might die, but all passed by without getting hurt.

---

1. Psalm 120:3–4

2. Judges 5:6–7

Chapter Twelve

Arrival at the Palace Beautiful

They could see the porter's lodge getting closer, so they hurried along, hoping to arrive before dark since traveling at night was dangerous. Great Heart knocked at the gate as soon as they arrived.

"Who's there?" the porter cried out.

"It is I," Great Heart called back. Instantly the porter came down because he recognized Great Heart's voice since he'd been there often as the conductor of pilgrims.

The porter came down to open the gate. "Hello, Mr. Great Heart! And what brings you here so late at night?" he asked, not seeing the women and children standing behind him.

"The Lord has commanded me to bring some pilgrims here to stay for a while," he replied, gesturing back. "I would have been here some time ago had the giant who used to assist the lions not opposed me. But I cut him down after a long and tedious fight and brought the pilgrims here safely."

"Will you come inside and stay until morning?" asked the porter.

"No," he said, shaking his head. "I'll be returning to my Lord tonight."

Christiana shot a quick glance over at Great Heart. "Oh, sir, I cannot believe you would leave us to travel alone without you! You've been faithful and loving to us and fought so bravely! Your counsel and wisdom have been so thoughtful. I'll never forget how good you've been to us."

Mercy did her best to plead with their faithful guide. "Oh, if you could just stay with us until the end of our journey! How can poor women like us stay on a highway so full of trouble like this one without a friend and defender?"

"Please, sir," James said, tears welling up in his small eyes, "what can we do to persuade you to stay and help us? We are weak, and the way is so dangerous."

"I'm at my Lord's command," said Great Heart, smiling kindly at his new friends. "If He had asked me to be your guide the entire way, I would willingly go with you. But you failed to ask Him from the start. Had you begged Him to have me guide you through to the end, He would have granted your request. But as it is, I must leave immediately." As he was turning to leave, he glanced back over his broad shoulders. "Goodbye, Christiana, Mercy, and my brave children."

The porter, whose name was Watchful, asked Christiana about her family and where she was from. "I'm a widow from the City of Destruction and my husband's name was Christian, the pilgrim."

"Really!" the porter said excitedly. "Christian was your husband?"

"Yes," she said proudly, "and these are his children. And this," she said pointing to Mercy. "is one of our neighbors."

The porter rang the bell, as he normally did in these situations, and a young woman named Humble-mind came to the door. "Go announce to those inside that Christiana, the wife of Christian, and her children have arrived on pilgrimage."

The young woman went and told the others that Christiana was at the door. No sooner had she made this announcement than they heard a wonderful celebration at the mention of her name!

Those inside the house hurried to the porter standing at the door with Christiana and said to her, "Come in, Christiana, come in, wife of that good man! Come in, blessed woman! Come in, all who are with you!" So she went in, followed by her children and Mercy.

They were led to an enormous room and asked to sit down while the leader of the house came in to welcome them. When others from the house arrived and were told who they were, they welcomed them with a kiss. "We welcome all of you who bear the grace of God!"

It was getting late, and Christiana, Mercy, and the boys were tired from the journey. Seeing Great Heart fight Grim and then passing by the terrible lions had left them shaken, so they asked to go rest as soon as possible.

"Soon," the family said, "but first refresh yourself with a little food." For they had prepared a lamb for them with the sauce that accompanied it.[1] The porter had heard they were coming and had earlier instructed those in the house to prepare for their arrival.

After eating and ending their prayer with a psalm, they once again asked to go rest. Christiana, though, had a special request. "If we may be so bold as to choose, can we please stay in the bedroom that my husband stayed in when he was here?" They agreed, and once settled in, Christiana and Mercy began discussing things they found interesting.

"When my husband went on a pilgrimage," Christiana whispered so as not to wake the boys, "I never would have thought I would have followed."

"And you also never thought you would be lying in the same room and in the same bed as he did to rest as you are now," replied Mercy.

Christiana shook her head and chuckled quietly. "Nor did I ever think I would feel comfortable seeing his face again and worshiping the Lord the King with him. Yet I believe I will now!"

Mercy placed a finger to her lips and made a shushing noise. "Listen! Do you hear that noise?"

Christiana listened carefully. "Yes, I believe it's the sound of music celebrating our arrival here."

"That's wonderful!" Mercy exclaimed. "Music in the house, music in the heart, and music also in heaven. I'm so happy we're here!" They talked for a while longer then fell asleep.

When they woke the next morning, Christiana asked Mercy, "Why did you laugh in your sleep last night? You must have been dreaming."

Mercy covered her mouth, quite embarrassed. "I guess I did...and what a sweet dream it was! But are you sure I laughed?"

"Yes," Christiana giggled, "you laughed with much enthusiasm. But please tell me, Mercy, what was your dream about?"

Mercy looked up at the ceiling and thought for a moment. "I dreamed I sat all alone in a quiet room and was upset about the hardness of my heart. I hadn't been there long when others gathered around me to hear what I was saying. As they listened, I continued crying out about the hardness of my heart, which just made them laugh at me, call me a fool, and then push me around. I looked up and saw someone with wings coming toward me, and when he reached me he said, 'Mercy, what's wrong?' I told him, and he said, 'Peace be with you.' He then wiped my eyes with his handkerchief and covered me with silver and gold.[2]

"He also put a chain around my neck, earrings in my ears, and a beautiful crown on my head. Then he took me by the hand and said, 'Mercy, follow me.' So I followed him as he went up until we arrived at a golden gate. When he knocked at the gate, it opened for him, and I then followed him into a throne room. The One who sat on the throne said to me, 'Welcome, daughter!' The place appeared bright and twinkling like the stars or, rather, like the sun. I thought I saw your husband there too. Then I woke from my dream." She paused and smiled softly to herself then added, "But did I really laugh in my sleep?"

Christiana raised both eyebrows and let out a great laugh. "Oh, you laughed all right!" She then laid a hand on Mercy's shoulder and became more thoughtful. "And why shouldn't you laugh when seeing yourself so adorned like you were? You must forgive me for saying so, but I believe this was a wonderful dream. You've already found the first part of the dream to be true, so in time, you'll find the second part true as well. Scripture tells us, 'For God speaks in one way or another, though man does not perceive it. In a dream, in a vision of the night, when deep sleep falls on men, while they slumber on their beds.'[3] We don't have to lie awake in bed waiting to hear from God. He can visit us while we sleep and cause us to hear His voice in our dreams. Our hearts are often awake while we are asleep, allowing God to speak to us just as well as if we were awake. And He does so by words, proverbs, signs, or however He wants."

Mercy's face was beaming with pleasure. "Well, I am glad for my dream, and I hope to see it fulfilled all the way to making me laugh again!"

"Well, I think it's about time that we get out of bed and figure out what we are supposed to do."

Mercy's face now grew concerned. "Please, if they invite us to stay awhile, let's willingly accept their offer. I would like to stay to grow better acquainted with these young women. I think Prudence, Piety, and Charity are very lovely and possess a clear-headed presence of mind."

Christiana agreed. "Let's see what they say." After they got dressed and came down, Prudence and Piety asked them how they rested and if they were comfortable or not.

"I rested very well!" Mercy said, not able to hide her smile. "It was one of the best night's sleeps that I've ever had in my life."

"Can we persuade you to stay here awhile?" asked Prudence and Piety. "You will have access to everything the house can provide you."

"Yes, we would be happy to stay!" said Christiana, smiling over at Mercy.

They agreed and stayed there for over a month or more, which was a spiritually enriching time for them.

---

1. Exodus 12:21, John 1:29
2. Ezekiel 16:8–11
3. Job 33:14–15

Chapter Thirteen

Prudence Talks to the Boys About Faith

Prudence could see how well Christiana had raised her children and asked for permission to speak with each of the boys about their faith. Christiana willingly consented, so Prudence began with the youngest, James.

"James, can you tell me who made you?" she asked with tenderness in her voice.

"God the Father, God the Son, and God the Holy Ghost," the young boy boldly replied.

"That's good," she said, smiling down at him in a reassuring way. "And can you tell me who saved you?"

James met her smile and nodded, answering the same: "God the Father, God the Son, and God the Holy Ghost."

"Very good again!" she said. "But can you tell me how the Father saves you?"

"He saved me by His grace."

"That's right," she said. Then, going a little deeper, she asked, "And how does God the Son save you?"

"He saved me by His righteousness, death and blood, and life."

"And finally," she asked, "how does God the Holy Ghost save you?"

James did not hesitate. "He saved me by revealing Himself to me, renewing me, and protecting me."

Prudence straightened her back and looked at Christiana with a knowing smile. "You're to be commended for how you've raised your children. I don't suppose I need to ask these same questions of the rest, since the youngest can answer them so well."

She then moved on to speak with the next youngest, named Joseph. "Can I talk to you about your faith, Joseph?"

"Absolutely!" he replied, though a little nervous.

"What is man?"

"Man is a rational creature made by God."

She nodded and then tilted her head to one side. "Why do you think a man needs to be saved?"

"He needs to be saved because of his sin—the same sin that put him into a state of captivity and misery."

"Yes," she said, nodding her approval again, "and why does a man need saving by the Trinity?"

Joseph thought for a moment before replying. "Because sin is so great and powerful a tyrant that no one can pull us out of its clutches but God. And God is so good and loving to man that He's willing to pull him out of his miserable state."

"What is God's purpose for these miserable men who become saved?" she asked.

"To bring glory to His name, His grace, and His justice, and more...not to mention the everlasting happiness of man!"

She asked Joseph one last question. "Then who can be saved?"

He smiled proudly. "Any who will accept His salvation."

"That's very good, Joseph," said Prudence with a cheerful look. "Your mother has taught you well, and you have listened to what she has told you."

Prudence then turned to Samuel, who was the second oldest. "Samuel, are you willing to talk with me about your faith?"

Samuel had eagerly been awaiting his turn. "Yes, definitely. Please do!"

"What is heaven?" she asked, looking directly at him.

"It's a blessed place and state of existence because it's where God lives," he said, feeling good about his answer.

She nodded and then, just as direct as before, followed up with, "And what is hell?"

Samuel frowned, troubled by the thought. "It's the most horrible place and state of existence because it's where sin, the devil, and death live."

"Tell me, Samuel," she asked, "why would you want to go to heaven?"

The boy's face brightened to a smile. "I want to go to heaven so that I may see God and serve Him without ever growing tired. And I want to see Christ and love Him forever while being full of the Holy Spirit. These are things I'm not able to fully enjoy now."

She smiled at him sweetly. "That's an excellent answer, Samuel. You've also learned well!"

Prudence then focused her attention on the oldest boy, Matthew. "Matthew, can I also talk to you about your faith?"

"Yes, I would be very happy to!" he replied excitedly.

"That's good," she said as the boy drew closer. "My first question for you is, did anything exist prior to God?"

"No," the elder boy replied, certain of his answer, "because God is eternal, and nothing but Him existed prior to the beginning of the first day. For in six days the Lord made heaven and earth, the sea, and all that is in them."

Her nod signaled he was correct. "How would you describe the Bible?"

"It is the holy Word of God," he replied.

"Is there anything in the Bible that you don't understand?"

Matthew leaned back against his chair and said truthfully, "Yes, a great deal, actually."

"When you come to a passage that you don't understand, what do you do?"

"I'm reminded that God is much wiser than I am, so I pray He will please help me understand what I'm reading for my benefit."

"What do you believe about the resurrection of the dead?" she asked.

"I believe the dead that have been buried will rise in the same nature but without corruption. And I believe this for two reasons: first, because God has promised it; and, second, because He can do it."

Then Prudence gathered the boys together and said, "You must still listen to your mother because she can teach you more. You must also diligently listen to the good things you hear from others because it is for your own benefit. Also, carefully observe what the heavens and earth teach you. But most importantly, mediate on that book, the Bible, that caused your father to become a pilgrim. As for me, I will teach you what I can while you are here with me. I will also be glad to answer any questions you have that lead to a clearer understanding of God's Word."

Chapter Fourteen

Mr. Brisk Visits Mercy

After spending a week at the Palace Beautiful, Mercy had a visitor named Mr. Brisk, who, by all accounts, liked her very much. He was a man from a reputable family who pretended to be religious but was more focused on the things of this world. Mercy was a beautiful woman, and Brisk was attracted to her, visiting often and telling her he loved her.

Mercy was the type of person who always kept herself busy doing something. When she had nothing to do, she would make clothes for others and give them to those in need. Mr. Brisk did not know what she was making or who she was giving it to, but he greatly admired the fact that she always seemed to work hard and was not idle. *I guarantee she'll make a good housewife*, he would say to himself.

Mercy decided it was time to tell the other young women who lived in the house about Mr. Brisk. She wanted to find out more about him since they knew him better than she did. They told her he was a very busy young man who pretended to be religious, but they feared he was unfamiliar with the power of anything good.

Mercy was emphatic in her response. "Well then, that settles it! I'll no longer consider him as a prospective husband, because I've determined never to place a burden on my soul."

"There's no need to spend a great deal of time trying to discourage him," Prudence advised with knowledge of the man. "Just continue the work you've been doing for the poor, and his pursuit of you will cool off quickly."

When Mr. Brisk visited again, he found her hard at work, as usual, making things for the poor. "Well, it seems like you're always working," he said, thinking her very industrious.

"Yes," she replied tersely, "I'm working hard for either myself or for others."

"Tell me, how much do you earn in a day?" he asked, keenly interested.

Mercy shook her head as she continued working. "I do these things so I may be rich in good works, storing up treasure for myself as a good foundation for the future so that I may take hold of that which is truly life."[1]

For a moment, he looked confused. Then he spoke disdainfully. "Well then, please tell me, what do you do with them?"

"I clothe the naked," she said, never looking up from her work.

After this encounter, his interest waned in the young woman, and he avoided coming to see her anymore. When asked the reason, he would say that "Mercy is a pretty woman but suffers from mental illness."

Once he had left, Prudence said to her, "Didn't I tell you that Mr. Brisk would soon abandon any interest he had in you? I have no doubt he will spread some nasty rumors about you, because despite his display of religion and his professed love for you, you two are of different minds—so different that I believe you could never come together."

"I've never told this to anyone," Mercy said, drawing in a deep breath, "but I could've been married before now. However, the men were all like Mr. Brisk in that we didn't think the same way, though none of them disparaged my character. We just couldn't agree on anything."

Seeing sadness in her eyes, Prudence warmly embraced her young friend. "Unfortunately, Mercy, today there are so many people who are just believers in name only—it's proven by their actions. I guess there are few who can truly live a godly life."

Mercy wiped a tear forming in the corner of her eye and smoothed out her dress before her. "Well, if nobody wants me as a wife, I'll die unmarried, or I'll be married to my beliefs. I cannot change who I am, and for as long as live, I intend never to marry a man who disagrees with me in this. I had a sister named Bountiful, who was married to one of these selfish people; they could never agree. But since my sister was determined to do as she always had, that is, to be kind to the poor, her husband publicly humiliated her first and then kicked her out of the house."

Prudence shook her head in disgust. "And yet I'm guessing he was a church member?"

"Yes, he was," she replied then added, "The world is full of such people, but I don't have need for any of them."

---

1. 1 Timothy 6:17–19

Chapter Fifteen

Matthew Falls Sick

It wasn't long before Christiana's oldest son, Matthew, became seriously ill with a stomachache. His illness was often so bad that it left him doubled over in pain. There was an older and well-known physician who lived nearby named Dr. Skill, whom Christiana sent for to come see her son.

Skill entered the room and, after quickly examining the boy, diagnosed him with severe gastric pain. "What has Matthew eaten lately?" he asked his mother, raising a critical eyebrow.

Christiana seemed shocked. "What has he eaten? Nothing but good food that I know of."

The doctor narrowed his eyes suspiciously at the boy. "He has eaten something that he shouldn't have, and it remains undigested in his stomach." Skill turned to address Christiana in a serious and direct tone. "Whatever it is, it will not go away on its own, and he will die unless it's removed."

Samuel interrupted softly, "Mother, what was it that Matthew gathered and ate as soon as we came through the gate onto the Way? If you remember, there was an orchard on the lefthand side of the wall with trees hanging over it. I believe he pulled down the branches and ate some of its fruit."

MATTHEW FALLS SICK 75

"You're right, Samuel!" she replied, her voice rising sharply. "He was not good that day and took some of that fruit. I scolded him, but he ate it anyway."

Skill nodded by way of affirmation. "I knew he had eaten something that wasn't good food. And that food, specifically that fruit, is the most harmful of all because it's the fruit from Beelzebub's orchard. I'm surprised you received no warning about the orchard. Many have died from its fruit."

Christiana began to cry. "Oh, he has been bad, and I'm a careless mother! What can I do for my son?"

"Come now," Skill said, trying to comfort her. "Don't be too worried. The boy may get well again, but he must purge whatever is in his stomach by vomiting."

A gleam of hope mixed with fear filled her eyes. "Please, sir, do whatever you can for him, whatever the cost."

Skill waved her off. "No, no, I'm sure it will be reasonable."

Now, physicians often give strange medicines to their patients. He made his first batch of medicine from goat's blood, the ashes of a calf, and juice from a hyssop plant.[1] It was to help induce vomiting but was too weak and didn't work for Matthew. Skill was determined to make a new batch. This one he gave the Latin name, *ex carne et sanguine Christi*, or from the body and blood of Christ.[2] He made the medicine into pills with a promise or two and a proportional quantity of salt.[3] Matthew was to take them three at a time while fasting and with a quarter pint of the tears of repentance.[4]

The medicine was prepared and brought to the boy. However, Matthew was afraid to take it even though he was in severe pain and his stomach felt like it was being torn apart from the inside.

The physician placed his hand behind Matthew's head. "Come, come, you must take it."

"It makes my stomach feel worse," the boy groaned.

Christiana's tone was desperate but adamant. "I must insist you take it."

Matthew placed his hands over his mouth. "But I will vomit it up again!"

"Tell me, sir," she asked, querying the capable doctor, "how does it taste?"

He shrugged his shoulders then said, "It doesn't taste bad."

Christiana touched one pill with the tip of her tongue. "Oh, Matthew!" she said, begging her son. "This medicine tastes sweeter than honey. If you love your mother, brothers, and Mercy—and if you love your life—you need to take it!"

After much fuss and a brief prayer asking God to bless it, he took the medicine, and it helped. It caused him to vomit, and then he fell asleep, resting quietly. Soon his fever broke, his breathing returned to normal, and his stomach pains were gone. In no time, he could get up and walk about the house with a cane. He would go from room to room, talking with Prudence, Piety, and Charity about his illness and how he had been healed.

Once Matthew was doing better, Christiana asked Dr. Skill, "Sir, what do I owe you for your time and care of my child?"

"According to the rules made in that case and provided, you must pay the Master of the College of Physicians," he replied.[5]

She nodded. "Tell me, what else is this pill good for?"

"It's a universal pill," he said, packing up his bag. "It's good to battle all the diseases that trouble pilgrims. And when it's prepared well, it will keep good forever."

"Please, sir, make me up twelve boxes of them because if I can get these, I'll never need another medicine."

Skill stopped packing momentarily to offer a warm smile to the desperate mother. "These pills are good for preventing diseases as well as curing the sick. And I'm confident that if a man uses this medicine as he should, he'll live forever.[6] But, Christiana, only administer this medicine in the way I've prescribed. Otherwise, they'll do no good."

He gave Christiana medicine for herself, the boys, and Mercy. He warned Matthew about eating green plums again then kissed each of them and went on his way.

As I said earlier, Prudence had told the boys that she would be happy to answer any questions they had. All they had to do was ask. After Matthew started feeling better, he went to ask her why medicine must taste so bad and why, when it worked, it caused him to vomit.

Prudence sat in a chair by a black hearth to face the young boy. "You see, Matthew, the bitter taste of medicine is often how a sinful heart responds to the Word of God. And just like vomiting empties your stomach, the Word cleanses the heart and mind. What medicine does for the body, the Word of God does for the soul."

Matthew nodded while gazing at the fire burning brightly in the fireplace. "What can we learn from seeing the flames of a fire rise and the sweet influence of sun's heat coming down?"

"When we see flames rise," she said, "we learn to ascend to heaven by passionate, fervent desires. And by the sun sending its heat and sweet influences down, we learn that the Savior of the world, though He was in heaven, reached down with His grace and love to us below."

The boy seemed to consider this then asked, "Well, where do clouds get their water from, and why do they empty themselves upon the earth?"

"Clouds get their water from the sea and then empty themselves upon a thirsty earth," Prudence replied. "In the same way, a minister should draw their own teaching from God and then give away what they've learned to the world."

"Why does the sun cause a rainbow?"

"To show that the promise of God's grace is confirmed to us in Christ."

"Why do springs come to us through the earth from the sea?"

"To show that the grace of God comes to us through the body of Christ," she said.

"Why do some springs rise out of the tops of high hills?"

"To show that the spirit of grace will spring up in some that are great and mighty as well as in many that are poor and humble."

Matthew nodded again. "Why does fire fasten itself upon the candle wick?"

"To show that unless grace kindles the heart, there will be no true light of life in us."

"But why is the wick and wax used up to maintain the light of the candle?"

"Ah," she said with a deep sigh, "that's helping us learn we should use our complete body and soul in the service of God, maintaining the light of His grace within us."

"Why does the pelican pierce her own breast with her bill?" he asked.

"To nourish her young ones with her own blood. In the same way, our blessed Christ loves His young—his people—so much as to save them from death by His blood."

"What can we learn from hearing a rooster's crow?"

She thought of the Apostle Peter. "We can learn from Peter's sin and grief. The rooster crowing reminds us that the day of judgment, that last and terrible day, is coming."

After about a month, Christiana told those in the house that it was time for them to be leaving.

---

1. Hebrews 9:13, 9:18, 10:1–4
2. John 6:54–57, Hebrews 9:14
3. Mark 9:49
4. Zechariah 12:10
5. Hebrews 13:11–15
6. John 6:51

Chapter Sixteen

Leaving the Palace Beautiful

"Don't forget to send a letter to Mr. Interpreter," Joseph suggested to his mother, thinking about their imminent departure. "I think it would be a good idea to ask him to send Mr. Great Heart back to guide us through the rest of our journey."

"Good boy," she said. "I had almost forgotten!" So Christiana wrote a letter and asked Mr. Watchful, the porter, to send it by some competent messenger to her good friend Mr. Interpreter.

After receiving and reading the letter, the Interpreter instructed the messenger, "Go, tell them I will send him."

As Christiana and her companions planned to leave, the family there called the entire house together and gave thanks to their King for sending such wonderful guests. "Christiana," they said to her, "it's our custom to show pilgrims something for them to think about as they travel along the Way."

They took Christiana, the boys, and Mercy into a small room and showed them the apple that Eve ate before giving it to her husband. It was the eating of this apple that turned them both out of Paradise. "What do you think this is?" they asked her.

Christiana looked closely. "It's either food or poison, but I'm not sure which." They told her the story, and she lifted her hands in praise.[1]

The family led them to another place, where they saw Jacob's ladder.[2] Christiana and those with her watched while angels climbed the ladder, and as they were leaving, James asked his mother, "Can we please stay here a while longer? I find this scene most interesting." So they turned around and stood there, staring at such an awesome sight.

Afterward, they were taken to a place where there was a golden anchor hung, and they asked Christiana to take it down. "It's absolutely necessary that you take this anchor with you. It provides hope and will keep you standing strong whenever you find yourself in turbulent weather."[3] The pilgrims were delighted with this news.

Next they took them to the mountain upon which our father Abraham offered his son, Isaac. They showed them the altar, the wood, the fire, and the knife that were used because they remain there to be seen to this very day.[4] After seeing these things, they held up their hands with praise, saying, "Oh! What a man Abraham was to deny himself for the love of his Master."

After they had showed them all these things, Prudence took them into the dining room, where there was an excellent harpsichord. She began playing, creating an excellent song out of all they had just seen. She sang, "We showed you Eve's apple, for which you should be aware. You saw Jacob's ladder too, on which the angels climbed. You've been given an anchor, but don't be satisfied until, like Abraham, you have given your best sacrifice."

It was around this same time that there was a knock at the door. The porter opened it to find Great Heart standing there, and suddenly the house was filled with great joy! It reminded everyone how, not so long ago, he had slain old Grim the giant and how he delivered them from the lions.

Great Heart said to Christiana and to Mercy, "My Lord has sent each of you a bottle of wine and some corn nuts and fruit to refresh you on your journey. He also sent figs and raisins for the boys."

They started on their journey, with Prudence and Piety walking alongside them as they approached the gate. "Have any other pilgrims traveled by lately?" Christiana asked the porter.

"No," he said, shaking his head, "there was only one some time back who told me of a great robbery that happened on the King's highway in the direction you're going. But he said they captured the thieves, and they will soon go to trial for their lives."

Christiana and Mercy became afraid, but Matthew said, "Mother, there's nothing to fear as long as Mr. Great Heart goes with us as our guide."

Christiana turned back to the porter. "Sir, I'm grateful for all the kindnesses you've shown to me since coming here. And I'm also thankful for your being so loving and kind to my children. I don't know how to repay all that you've done. Therefore, I ask that you accept this small token of my appreciation for you," she said, placing a gold angel in his hand.

He bowed low in admiration. "Let your clothes always be white and your head never needing medicine. Let Mercy live forever and her work be plenty." To the boys, he said, "Run from youthful passions and pursue godliness with those who are serious and wise. In this way, you will make your mother's heart glad and will find praise from all who are knowledgeable."[5] They thanked the porter once more then left.

Now I saw in my dream that they started walking until they came to the top of the hill, and then Piety cried out, "Dear me! I forgot to bring what I intended to give to Christiana and her companions. I'll go back and get it." And she ran back to the house.

While she was gone, Christiana thought she heard in a grove a little way off on the righthand side of the Way the most interesting and sweet-sounding music. The words sounded like, "Through all my life your favor has been so openly shown to me and I will live in your house forever."

As she continued listening, she thought she heard another answer, saying, "And why? Because the Lord our God is good; His mercy guaranteed; His truth always stands firm and has endured throughout time."

Christiana asked Prudence what made that sweet and interesting music.[6] "Those are our country birds," she said, with a glance up into the trees. "They only sing these notes in the spring, when the flowers appear and the sun is shining warmly. Then you may hear them all day long. I often go out to hear them, and we even keep them tame in our house. They're wonderful company for us when we're sad, but they also make the woods, groves, and quiet places desirable to be in."

By this time, Piety had returned. "Look here!" she said excitedly to Christiana. "I've brought you a diagram of all those things that you've seen at our house. When you find yourself forgetful, you can look at it and remember for teaching and comfort."

---

1. Genesis 3:6, Romans 7:24
2. Genesis 28:12
3. Hebrews 6:19, Joel 3:16
4. Genesis 22:9
5. Ecclesiastes 9:8, Deuteronomy 33:6, 2 Timothy 2:22
6. Song of Solomon 2:11–12

Chapter Seventeen

The Valley of Humiliation

As they walked down the hill and into the Valley of Humiliation, they found it steep and slippery, but they were very careful and reached the bottom with little difficulty. When they entered the valley, Piety turned to Christiana. "This valley is where your husband, Christian, met the evil beast Apollyon and where they had that dreadful fight. I know you've heard the story, but stay strong because as long as you have Great Heart as your guide, we believe you'll do fine." Prudence and Piety then placed the care of the pilgrims into the hands of their guide and returned home.

Great Heart could tell they were nervous as he led them forward into the valley. "There's no need to be afraid of this valley, because nothing will hurt us here unless we bring it about ourselves. Yes, it's true that Christian met Apollyon here and that the beast bruised him up in battle, but that fight resulted from his slipping when he came down the hill. Anyone who slips on the hill will find a battle here. This is why the valley has gotten such a bad name.

"When the average man hears about such terrible things happening in a place like this, they're convinced it's now haunted with some evil beast or spirit. But nothing could be further from the truth! Instead, anything that happens here is actually the result of their own doing. The Valley of Humiliation is really as fruitful a place as any other over which the crow flies. I'm sure that if we just looked around, we might find some clue to explain why Christian had such a hard time here."

"Look!" James said to his mother, pointing ahead on the path. "There's a monument over there, and it looks like there's writing on it." They walked over and found written on the monument, "Let Christian's slips before he got here and the battles he faced when he arrived be a warning to those who come after."

"Now see there!" Their guide nodded confidently at the monument. "I told you that if we looked around, we would find some sign why Christian had such a hard time here."

Great Heart wondered if Christiana might now feel some disappointment in her husband. He placed his hand on her shoulder. "This is not a criticism of Christian or any others that have suffered the same misfortune he did coming through here. It's easier going up a hill than down, and you can't say that about many hills in this part of the world. Your husband was a good and brave man who had victory over his enemy and now is at rest. May God grant we will fare no worse when it's our turn to be tried."

He turned his attention back to the group. "But we will come back again to this Valley of Humiliation. It's one of the most fruitful and fertile grounds in all these parts, with many meadows. If a man happened to come here in the summer, as we have now, and knew nothing about the valley's past, he might think it's the most beautiful place he's ever seen. Just look at how green this valley is and how it's adorned with beautiful lilies![1]

"I've known many working men who have magnificent estates in this Valley of Humiliation because God resists the proud but gives grace to the humble.[2] There's no doubt that this valley has very fertile soil and can produce an abundant crop. Of course, there are others that no longer wish to be troubled by going over hills or mountains. Instead, they would rather enter their Father's house in this valley. But the Way is the Way, and there is an end."

Now, as they were traveling along and talking, they spotted a boy dressed in dirty clothes feeding his father's sheep, but he had a fresh and pleasing appearance. He sat by himself and sang.

Great Heart alerted the others to listen to what the shepherd boy was singing. They listened and heard him sing, "You don't need to fear falling when you are already low, and those who are low are not prideful. The one who is humble will always have God as his guide. I'm content with what I have, whether it is little or much. And, Lord, I still crave contentment because you saved me much. To be full is such a burden to those going on a pilgrimage. It's best to have a little here and then later bliss in the afterlife."

"Do you hear him?" asked their guide. "I venture to say this boy lives a happier life with a heart more at ease than one dressed in silk and velvet."

They continued walking as Great Heart recounted the story of the valley. "Our Lord used to have His country house in this valley. He loved being here and walking in the meadows, finding the air pleasant. And the valley is where a man can be free from the noise and distractions of life, whereas all other lands are full of noise and confusion. Only the Valley of Humiliation is an empty and quiet place where a man is not so preoccupied and hindered by his thoughts as he would normally be in other places. Nobody walks in the valley unless they love the pilgrim's life. Yes, Christian had the terrible misfortune of finding Apollyon here and confronting the beast in vigorous combat, but you must also understand that in the past, men have met with angels here, found pearls here, and found the words of life in this place.[3]

"Like I said, in the past, the Lord loved to walk in the valley when He had his country house here. In fact, He left a sum of money that is faithfully paid annually to all those who love treading these grounds. It's paid out to them during certain seasons to support them along the Way and to encourage them to continue their pilgrimage."

"Sir, I understand my father battled Apollyon in this valley, but where exactly was the battle fought?" James asked their brave guide, looking about. "It's such a large valley."

"Your father battled Apollyon at a place just ahead of us in the valley. It's in a narrow passage just beyond Forgetful Green, considered one of the most dangerous places in all these parts. This is because whenever a pilgrim meets with any opposition there, they forget everything good that's happened to them and how unworthy they are to receive any of it to begin with. There are others that have also struggled in the same place, but we'll talk more about it when we get there. For as I understand it myself, to this day there remains either some sign of the battle or some monument to testify that they fought such a battle."

Mercy, surprised at how at ease she felt, said, "I feel as good in this valley as I have anywhere else that we've traveled. I think this place suits my spirit best because I love to be where there are no rattling coaches or rumbling wheels. I also think that with just a little effort, one can spend time here considering who they are, where they came from, what they've done, and what the King has called them to do. Here one can think with a broken heart and a yielded spirit until their eyes become like the pools in Heshbon, pouring out tears.[4] Here also, where they can go through difficult and painful places in life, they become strengthened as God sends down rain from heaven to fill those pools. In this valley, the King will give His vineyards to those who are His, and they will go through it singing like Christian did even after meeting Apollyon."[5]

"That is true," their guide said, smiling. "I've gone through this valley many times and have never been better than when I was here. Many of the pilgrims I've guided through the valley have also said the same thing. The King says He will look graciously on those who have a poor and contrite spirit and who tremble at His Word."[6]

They continued walking until arriving at the place where Christian had fought his battle. Great Heart said to the group, "This is where Christian stood his ground, and up there is where Apollyon came down to attack him. And look," he said, pointing to a rock on the ground. "Didn't I tell you? Here remains some of your husband's blood on these stones to this very day."

Great Heart then motioned all around them. "If you look around, you can also see fragments of Apollyon's broken darts and how the two of them trampled around in the dirt, fighting to gain solid ground on the other. Also, look how their side blows split these very stones. Truly Christian proved himself as strong and brave a man as Hercules. After Apollyon's defeat, he retreated to the next valley, called the Valley of the Shadow of Death. We will arrive there soon." Great Heart pointed to a monument across the other side of the Way. "And look over there. It is the monument commemorating Christian's battle, his victory, and his fame throughout history."

They walked over to it and read the writing, which said, word for word, "It was in this place that Christian and Apollyon fought a hard and extraordinary battle, trying to overcome one another. I stand on this monument to testify that the man was brave and made the beast fly away."

After passing through the Valley of Humiliation, they came to the border of the Valley of the Shadow of Death.

---

1. Song of Solomon 2:1

2. James 4:6, 1 Peter 5:5
3. Hosea 12:4–5, Matthew 13:46, Proverbs 8:36
4. Song of Solomon 7:4
5. Psalm 84:5–7, Hosea 2:15
6. Isaiah 66:2

Chapter Eighteen

The Valley of the Shadow of Death

The Valley of the Shadow of Death was longer than the other valley and a place many believed strangely haunted and evil. But since they had Great Heart as a guide and because it was still daylight, the pilgrims were passing through it better than expected.

As they entered the valley, they heard a considerable amount of groaning, like that of dying men. The groaning seemed to express words of grief as if in some extreme torment. The sounds shook the boys and the women looked pale and weak, but their guide encouraged them not to worry.

Traveling a little farther, they felt the ground beneath them shake, as though someone had hollowed it out. They also heard a hissing noise, like that of snakes, but saw nothing. The boys, still shaken, said, "Are we not at the end of this miserable place yet?" Great Heart once again encouraged them all to be brave and careful where they walked. There were many snares in this valley, and they wouldn't want to chance falling into one.

James began to feel sick, but I think it was more because he was frightened. His mother gave him a drink from the bottle she had received from the Interpreter and three of the pills Dr. Skill had prepared. In no time, the boy felt better, and they continued their journey until coming to about the middle of the valley.

"I think I see something on the road there in front of us," Christiana said, squinting to make out what it was. "I've seen nothing quite like it!"

"Mother, what is it?" James asked nervously.

She shook her head with a mixture of fear and disbelief. "An ugly thing, child, an ugly thing..."

"But, Mother, what is it like?" he asked again, almost at a whisper.

"I can't tell what it is," she replied, trying to stay calm, but her quivering lips gave her away. "And now it's getting closer—much closer!"

"Well, well," said Great Heart, carefully eyeing the approaching fiend. "If you're afraid, stay close to me."

The fiend came close, and the guide met it. But just as it looked poised to attack, it vanished before their eyes. It reminded them of the saying, "Resist the devil, and he will flee from you."[1] After this, they felt better as they continued through the valley.

It wasn't long, though, before Mercy thought she saw what appeared to be a lion behind them. The roar it made when it came running up on them was so loud it made the entire valley echo. Their hearts all sank—all, that is, except for the heart of their guide as he placed himself between the fierce, approaching lion and the pilgrims. The lion came on fast, and Great Heart prepared himself for battle.[2] But when the lion could tell Great Heart was determined to resist, it drew back and came no farther.

They continued again with their guide leading them until they came to a great pit in the road. They estimated it to be the width of the entire valley. But before they could prepare themselves to cross over, a great fog and darkness fell upon them, and they could not see.

THE VALLEY OF THE SHADOW OF DEATH 91

"Oh no!" the pilgrims gasped, trying to make out the road before them. "What should we do now?"

Great Heart did his best to calm their nerves. "Don't be afraid. Just be patient, and let's see how this all works out in the end."

The blocked path kept them where they were. While there, they could clearly hear the movements of their enemies and see the fire and the smoke from the pit.

Christiana turned to Mercy. "Now I see what my poor husband went through. I've heard a lot about this place, but I've never been here before now. Poor man! To think he came through here all alone at night in the dark, and it was dark for most of his way. Also, these bustling fiends were all around him, ready to tear him to pieces at any minute. Many have talked about it, but no one really knows what the Valley of the Shadow of Death is like until they enter it themselves. The heart knows its own bitterness, and no stranger shares its joy.[3] It's a fearful thing to be here."

Great Heart stroked his beard contemplatively. "This valley is like doing business in deep waters, deep in the heart of the sea. Or you could say it's like going down to the base of the mountains. But when it seems like the barriers of the earth will surround you forever—and you're walking in darkness and with no light—trust in the name of your Lord and stay close to God."[4]

He then added by way of setting their minds at ease, "As I've told you already, I, too, have gone through this valley many times with much more difficulty than I am right now. Yet you can see that I'm alive. I'm not saying this to boast in any way, because I cannot save myself. But because of my experience, I now trust that deliverance will come. Come, let's pray to the One who can shine light into our darkness and rebuke not just these fiends but all the devils in hell."

They desperately cried out and prayed to God, and He sent light and deliverance. The path before them was now clear and the pit filled, but they were not through the valley yet.

They continued walking but found the foul odor and disgusting smells overwhelming. Mercy said to Christiana with a wry smile, "It's not nearly as pleasant here as it was at the gate!" She added, "Or, for that matter, at the Interpreter's house or at the Palace Beautiful."

"Oh, but it's not as bad to go through here as it would be to live here forever," said Samuel. "And for all we know, maybe the reason we must travel this way is that the home being prepared for us will be that much sweeter when we arrive."

"Well said, Samuel!" their guide chimed in, smiling. "You're speaking like a man now."

Samuel returned the smile and seemed to stand taller. "Why, if ever I get out of here, I think I will cherish light and good much more than I ever have before."

Great Heart nodded as he continued to lead them through the valley. "We will be out soon enough."

The journey continued for some time, until Joseph became exasperated, saying, "How come we can't see the end of this valley yet?"

Great Heart didn't answer the boy directly; instead, he gestured at the road in front of them. "Watch your step as we will soon be among the snares."

They were careful to watch every step, but many of the snares still worried them. After passing through that area, they saw a man thrown into the ditch on the lefthand side of the road. His flesh was all ripped and torn.

"That man's name was Heedless," their guide said, shaking his head. "He was going through the valley but has laid there for a long time. There was another man, named Take-heed, who was with him when they captured and killed him, but he escaped their hands. You cannot imagine how many people they've killed in this area. Yet so many are foolish enough to venture out casually on a pilgrimage without a guide. Poor Christian! It's a wonder he escaped this place at all. But his heart was good, and God loved him or else he never could have passed through."

As they drew near the end of the valley where Christian had passed by the giant's cave, another giant, named Maul, came forward. This giant was in the habit of destroying young pilgrims by deceiving them. He shouted out to the pilgrims' guide by name: "Great Heart! How many times have you been warned not to do these things?"

"What things?" Great Heart replied, placing one hand on his sheathed sword.

"What things!" the giant roared with fury. "You know what things, but I'll put an end to your trade."

"Very well, but before we start, let's make sure we understand the reason for our fighting," he said as the women and children stood by trembling, not knowing what to do.

The giant broke out irritably, "Because you rob this valley and are the worst of thieves!"

Great Heart leaned back his head and laughed. "But these are just but random accusations. Tell me, man, what specific robberies have I committed?"

Maul leveled an enormous finger right at the guide and growled, "You're a kidnapper! You gather up women and children and carry them off to a strange country. Your theft weakens my master's kingdom."

Great Heart cast a fierce gaze in the direction of his opponent. "I'm a servant of the God of heaven, and my business is to persuade sinners to repent. I'm commanded to do my best to turn men, women, and children from darkness to light and from the power of Satan to God. If this, in fact, is the reason for our quarrel, let's begin this battle as soon as you're ready."

Then the giant stepped forward, and Great Heart went to meet him. In their approach, the brave guide drew his sword and the giant his club. Exchanging no more words, they began fighting. The giant struck the first blow, knocking Great Heart down on one knee. He fell so quickly that it alarmed the women and children, and they cried out. But Great Heart recovered and stood back up, attacking his enemy with brute force and wounding the giant in the arm. The battle continued like this for the better part of an hour. At one point the fighting became so heated that the breath coming from the giant's nostrils was like heat from a boiling cauldron.

They both took a break to sit down and rest. Great Heart prayed while the women and children did nothing but sigh and cry the entire time the battle lasted. After resting and catching their breath, they resumed fighting, and with one blow, Great Heart knocked the giant down to the ground.

"No!" the giant yelled, raising his hand. "Hold up and let me recover!"

Great Heart stood his ground but was fair and let Maul stand back up before they went at it again. This time, the giant narrowly missed breaking Great Heart's skull with his club.

After that, Great Heart could take no more and ran at him with everything he had in his spirit, piercing the giant under the fifth rib. Maul fell to the ground and was weak, unable to hold up his club anymore. Great Heart landed his final blow, cutting off the giant's head from his shoulders.

With the battle over, the women and children rejoiced, and Great Heart praised God for delivering him. Afterward, the pilgrims erected a monument and placed the giant's head on it. They wrote a message underneath for traveling pilgrims that read, "The giant who once wore this head deceived pilgrims by blocking their way. He spared none and abused all until I, Great Heart, came forward to be the pilgrim's guide to oppose him who was their enemy."

Now I saw as they were ascending to higher ground, there was a place set up not too far off to offer pilgrims a clear view ahead of them. It was the same place Christian had first spotted his brother, Faithful. For this reason, when they finally arrived, they sat down to rest, eat, drink, and celebrate God delivering them from such a dangerous enemy. As they sat eating, Christiana asked their guide if he had been wounded from the battle.

"Nothing except small bodily wounds," said Great Heart, surveying his cuts, scrapes, and bruises inflicted from the battle. "Yet any pain I have is nothing compared to the proof it presents of the love I have for my Master and for you. By God's grace, it will be a means to increase my reward in the end."

Christiana took a drink and tilted her head to the side. "But weren't you afraid when you saw him come out with his club?"

Great Heart merely shrugged as he took a bite of pomegranate. "It is my duty not to trust my own abilities but to trust in Him who is stronger than all."

She considered that answer then countered, "Yes, but what were you thinking when he knocked you to the ground with that first blow?"

"Well," the brave guide responded, shrugging again, "I remembered they had served my Master blows, and yet He conquered in the end."[5]

Matthew had been listening to the conversation and cut in. "While you all can think what you please, I think God has been wonderfully good to us. He has brought us out of this valley and delivered us from the hand of our enemy. As for me, I see no reason to distrust our God anymore. In such a terrible place like this, He has given us proof of His love." They all agreed and got up to continue their journey.

---

1. James 4:7
2. 1 Peter 5:8–9
3. Proverbs 14:10
4. Isaiah 50:10
5. 2 Corinthians 4:10–11, Romans 8:37

Chapter Nineteen

Old Honest and Mr. Fearing

Before too long, they arrived at an oak tree where they found an old pilgrim sound asleep underneath it. They knew he was a pilgrim by his clothes, his staff, and the belt he wore around his waist. When Great Heart tried to wake the old gentleman, he opened his eyes and became startled. "What's the matter? Who are you, and what's your business here?" he cried out.

Great Heart held up his hands. "Calm down, man! Don't get so worked up. We're only friends." But the old man stood up and was on his guard until he knew better who they were.

"My name is Great Heart," the guide said and then motioned toward his companions, "and I'm guiding these pilgrims to the Celestial Country."

The old man began to let his guard down some. "You'll have to forgive me, but I was afraid you were part of the same group that robbed Little Faith's money some time back. But now that I'm awake and aware of my surroundings, I can tell you're honest people."

Great Heart smiled at the tenacity of the old man. "Well, I'm curious. What would you have done to protect yourself had we, in fact, been robbers?"

"What would I have done?" he said, instinctively placing his hand on his sword. "Why, I would have fought you for as long as there was breath in me. And if I had done just so, I'm sure you could never have bested me, because you cannot overcome a Christian unless he surrenders himself."

"Well said and very honest," agreed the guide. "From what you just said, I know you're the right kind of man because you have told the truth."

The old man nodded his appreciation. "I can also tell that you understand what a true pilgrimage is. You know, everyone else believes pilgrims are the quickest to be overcome."

"Well, now that we have so happily met, please tell me your name and where you are from."

The old man hesitated. "I cannot tell you my name, but I'm from the town of Stupidity that is just beyond the City of Destruction."

"Oh! You're that countryman?" Great Heart said with a knowing nod and smile. "Then I believe I have a good idea who you are. Your name is old Honesty, is it not?"

He blushed, appearing conflicted, and at last gave a brief nod. "Not Honesty in the philosophical sense but, yes, my name is Honest. And I wish my nature agreed with my name. But, sir," he asked curiously, "how did you know who I am?"

"My Master has told me about you," the guide replied. "He knows everything done on the earth. I've often wondered if any pilgrims have come from your town because, as you know, the City of Stupidity is worse than the City of Destruction."

"Yes, it's true that our town is farther from the sun, so we're colder and more senseless. But even if man were a mountain of ice, his frozen heart would start to thaw if the Sun of Righteousness should shine on him. This is what happened to me."

Great Heart nodded approvingly. "I believe it, father Honest. I believe it because I know it to be true."

Then the old gentleman greeted all the pilgrims with a holy kiss of love, asking them their names and how they had fared since setting out on their pilgrimage.

Christiana went first, telling Honest who she was. "I suppose you've heard of my name. Christian was my husband, and these are his four children."

You can't imagine how the old gentleman responded to the news of who she was. He skipped, he smiled, and he blessed them with a thousand good wishes. "I've heard a lot about your husband's journey and of the battles he fought in his days," he said, clasping his hands together joyfully. "Rest assured, your husband's name reverberates all over this part of the world. His faith, courage, endurance, and his sincerity above all have made his name famous."

He then turned to the boys and asked each one their names, which they told him. He approached Matthew first, saying, "Matthew, you're like Matthew the tax collector, not in wickedness but in honor and integrity."[1]

He then turned to Samuel. "Samuel, you're like Samuel the prophet, a man of faith and prayer."[2] And to Joseph he said, "You're like Joseph in Potiphar's house, pure and one who runs from temptation."[3] Finally, he turned to James and said, "And James, you're like James the Just and James the brother of our Lord."[4]

The boys told him about Mercy and how she had left her town and family to join them and their mother on their journey.

"So Mercy is your name?" Honest smiled, asking rhetorically. "Well, by mercy you will be sustained and carried through all the difficulties that assault you until you arrive at the place where you look directly at the Fountain of Mercy with comfort." Great Heart smiled and was pleased as he watched Honest converse with the pilgrims.

As they walked along together, the guide asked the old gentleman if he knew a man named Mr. Fearing, who came on a pilgrimage to this area.

"Yes, I knew him very well," Honest said, nodding. "He was a man who possessed the essence of faith but was also the most troubled pilgrim I've ever met in my life."

"Then it sounds like you did know him!" he said, grunting a humorless laugh. "I only say that because you've so accurately described his character."

"Oh, sure, I knew him!" he said. "Why, I was one of his best friends and was with him mostly near the end of his life. I was also with him when he began to think what would happen after this life."

Great Heart sighed as he continued walking. "I was his guide from my Master's house all the way to the gates of the Celestial City."

"Ah...then you knew him as a troubled man too?" Honest said, running his fingers through his long white beard.

The guide nodded. "Oh yes, but I handled it fairly well. You see, people like Fearing often find themselves entrusted to men of my calling."

"Interesting!" Honest said. "Can you tell us how he managed under your guidance?"

Great Heart's stride slowed as he recounted the story of Mr. Fearing. "Well, he was always afraid of falling short wherever he wanted to go. Everything frightened him, especially if there was the slightest hint of opposition. I heard he laid around in a deep depression at the Swamp of Despair for over a month. He watched many cross over before him but wouldn't dare risk it himself, even though many offered to lend him a hand.

"But he was also adamant not to return home. He said he would rather die than not go to the Celestial City. Yet with every challenging situation, he became discouraged, and he struggled with every minor hindrance that anyone threw his way.

"As I said, he stayed at the Swamp of Despair for a long time, until one sunny morning, he ventured over. I have no idea how he did it, and once he made it over, he couldn't believe it himself. I think the swamp occupied all his thoughts. He must have carried it with him all the time, or he wouldn't have been so afraid of everything."

The others were now walking close to their guide, listening intently to his story.

"Fearing eventually arrived at the gate—you know the gate I'm referring to, the one at the head of the Way. Well, he stood there for a long time before he found the courage to knock. And when they opened the gate, he would step back, saying he was unworthy. Many others went in before him, even though he had arrived before they did. The poor man would stand there shaken and frightened. I dare say anyone who saw him would have felt terrible for the man. But even in his fear, he still refused to go back.

"Finally he took the hammer that was hanging on the gate and gave it a small knock or two. But when the gate opened, he stepped back like before. Except this time, the One who opened the gate came forward and asked, 'Scared one, what do you want?' which only made Fearing fall to the ground. The One who spoke wondered why the man seemed so weak. He told him, 'Don't be afraid. Get up because I've opened the door for you. Come in, blessed one.'

"Fearing was still trembling, but he got up and walked through the gate, ashamed to show his face once inside. They showed him their traditional hospitality until it was time for him to be on his way. Then they advised him what to take with him as he left."

The group ambled along as their guide's steady gaze remained constantly on the path in front of them.

"Fearing walked until he arrived at my master the Interpreter's house and behaved in much the same way at the door as he had at the gate. He laid around in the cold for a good while before he dared to do anything. Yet he still refused to turn and go home, even though the nights were long and cold back then. This is all despite the fact that he kept a note in his chest pocket addressed to my Master about his fear. The note said to receive the man and grant him everything the house had to offer. But the note also said to provide Fearing a strong and brave guide because he himself was so chicken-hearted.

"Yet even with that note securely in his chest pocket, he was afraid to knock at the door. Instead, he hung around until he was about starved, watching others knock and get in. His fear was so paralyzing that he was afraid to risk it himself.

"Finally I looked out the window and saw a man lying around by the door. I went out to him and asked who he was, but all the poor man could do was cry. I then understood what he wanted and went back into the house and told the others as well as explained the situation to our lord. He sent me out to invite him in again, but I tell you, it wasn't easy. Finally he came in, and my lord was wonderful and loving to him. There wasn't much food left on the table, but what there was, the Master placed on Fearing's plate.

"Then he presented the note to my Lord, who read it and then granted his request. After being there a good while, Fearing seemed to get braver and even a little more comfortable. As you know, my master has a very tender heart, especially for those who are afraid, so he tried to encourage the man as much as he could.

"Well, after he had seen the things of the house and was ready to take his journey to the Celestial City, Fearing was given a bottle of spirits and some good food to eat by my lord—just as he did with Christian. This is how the two of us began our journey, with me walking before him, guiding him along the Way. He was a man of few words, although I could hear him sighing aloud as we walked.

"When we came to the place where they hung those three fellows, Fearing said he didn't believe he would meet the same fate. He seemed glad when he saw the cross and the tomb and wanted to stay there awhile to look at it. I'll admit, it seemed to cheer him up. Interestingly enough, he didn't hesitate at the Hill of Difficulty nor was he really afraid of the lions. It's hard to explain, but he didn't fear things like that. His fear was more about his being accepted at the end of his journey.

"I think I got him to the Palace Beautiful before he really wanted to be there. When I introduced him to the young women of the house, he seemed too ashamed to join in with their company. He mostly desired to be alone unless there was a discussion of spiritual matters. Then he would hide behind something and listen. He also really loved to see ancient things and to think about them. But it was some time later that he told me he mostly loved being at the Gate and at the Interpreter's house. Unfortunately, while there, he didn't have the courage to ask about either of them.

"We left the Palace Beautiful and went down the hill into the Valley of Humiliation. Amazingly, he went down just as well as I've ever seen in my life. It was like he was finally happy and didn't have a care in the world. There seemed to be some kind of bond between him and that valley because I never saw him better in all his pilgrimage than when he was there. He would lie down and embrace the ground, kissing the very flowers that grew there.[5] Then he would rise every morning at the crack of dawn, walking back and forth, exploring the valley."

The glow that had lit up Great Heart's face now faded as his tone became more serious. "But when it came time to enter the Valley of the Shadow of Death, I thought I might lose him. Not that he had any inclination to go back, for he always despised the idea. Rather, the valley scared him to death. He would cry out, 'Oh, the hobgoblins will get me! The hobgoblins will get me!' I couldn't convince him otherwise. He made such a racket there that had any hobgoblins heard him, it was encouragement enough to come and attack us.

"But I noticed as we walked through the valley, it seemed quieter than I've ever experienced, either before or since. I supposed our Lord restrained those enemies and commanded them not to intervene until Fearing had passed through the valley.

"His entire story is much too long to tell, so I'll just mention a couple more things. The first is when he came to Vanity Fair. I thought he was going to fight every man at the fair. I actually feared he would get us both killed as heated as he got about their foolishness. Then, at the Enchanted Ground, he was very alert, but when seeing no bridge at the river, he once again became paralyzed with fear. He thought he would drown forever, never seeing that face with peace that he had come so many miles to see.

"It was here again that I noticed something quite remarkable. The water in the river was the lowest I'd ever seen it in my entire life. Fearing finally crossed over, barely getting his feet wet! When he was going up to the gate, I told him goodbye and wished him a good reception above. 'I will, I will,' he replied. Then we parted ways, and I never saw him again."

Honest was excited to hear the news about his old friend. "Then it seems, in the end, everything went well for him!"

"Oh yes!" said Great Heart. "I had no doubts about him. He had an exceptional spirit, but it was his depression and fear that made life difficult for him and for others.[6] Compared to some, though, he seemed more aware of his own sinfulness but also would deny himself something that was good because he thought it might hurt or offend others."[7]

The old man squinted up at the guide. "What could possibly be the reason that such a good man lived most of his life in fear?"

Great Heart shrugged. "Well, there are a couple of reasons. For one, God, in His wisdom, wants it that way. Think about it like children playing in the marketplace. There are some playing instruments for dancing and others singing sad songs. In this scenario, Mr. Fearing would be one playing the bass instrument while others like him are playing the trombone. Both instruments produce notes that are more depressing than notes of other instruments.[8]

"There are some that say the bass is the foundation of all music. As for me, I don't care at all for a profession of faith that doesn't start with deep, mindful sorrow. The fact is, the first string a musician usually touches when he intends to put all in tune is the bass. God also plays upon this string first when He sets the soul in tune for Himself. The only problem with Fearing is that he couldn't play anything but depressing music until the latter part of his life."

(I'm using a colorful metaphor here to help grow the intelligence of young readers, but also because the book of Revelation compares the saved to a company of musicians playing on their trumpets and harps, singing their songs before the throne.)[9]

"It's clear to anyone who hears his story that Mr. Fearing was a very passionate man," said Honest. "He didn't fear difficulties, lions, or Vanity Fair. Instead, it was only sin, death, and hell that terrorized him, and this was because he had concerns about his share in the Celestial Country."

"You're right." Great Heart nodded his agreement. "Those were the things that troubled him. And as you can see, those fears came from a weak mind, not from a weak spirit, which is the most authentic element of a pilgrim's life. Mr. Fearing is like the man in the proverb who would bite into a burning piece of wood if it stood in his way. But the things that oppressed him no man has ever shaken off easily."

Christiana had been listening to the exchange and said thoughtfully, "The story of Mr. Fearing has been good for me to hear because I thought nobody was like me. But then, after hearing his story, I see some similarities between that good man and myself...although with a couple of differences. First, his fear was so great that it was clear to all around him, whereas I kept mine hidden. Second, his fear was so paralyzing that it left him unable to knock at the doors of houses that could show him hospitality, but my fear just made me knock even louder."

"I would like to say something that's on my heart," Mercy said, interjecting. "After hearing this story, I, too, am a little like Mr. Fearing in that I've always been more afraid of the lake and losing a place in Paradise than of losing other things. Oh, I've often thought of how happy I would be to have a home there! It's enough to make me give up everything in this world to have it!"

"I've battled fear in my life too," Matthew piped in. "Fear led me to believe I wasn't saved—that I didn't have the assurance that accompanies salvation. But if a good man like Mr. Fearing struggled with the same fear and it went well for him, why would it not go well for me too?"

"With any fear comes the opportunity for grace," James said ardently. "Even though the one who fears hell might not always find grace, you can be absolutely sure there's no grace for the one who doesn't fear God."

"Well said, James," Great Heart said, beaming at the young boy. "You've hit the mark! For the fear of God is the beginning of wisdom, and to be sure, those that don't fear God will never attain wisdom in the end. But as we wrap up our story of Mr. Fearing, let's offer a farewell to this good man. Well, Mr. Fearing, you feared God and were afraid to do anything while here that would betray you. And even though you feared the lake and pit, others have too, but they were at a disadvantage, not having your intelligence."

---

1. Matthew 10:3

2. Psalm 99:6
3. Genesis 39
4. Acts 1:13
5. Lamentations 3:27–29
6. Psalm 88
7. Romans 14:12, 1 Corinthians 8:13
8. Matthew 11:16–18
9. Revelation 5:8, 14:2–3

Chapter Twenty

Mr. Self Will

Great Heart had no sooner finished telling his story of Mr. Fearing than Honest launched into his own story about a man he once knew named Mr. Self Will.

"That man just pretended to be a pilgrim," recalled Honest with stinging rebuke echoing in his voice. "I'm convinced he never entered at the gate that stands at the beginning of the Way."

Great Heart shook his head in disappointment. "Did you ever talk to him about it?"

"Oh yes, more than a couple of times," Honest nodded, "but it was always like him to be self-willed, doing whatever he wanted. He didn't care what others thought about him or whether he should set a good example. And he certainly didn't care about debating right or wrong. Self Will always did what he wanted to do, and nothing else would convince him otherwise."

"What principles did he live his life by?" asked Great Heart curiously. "It sounds like you knew him well enough to tell."

Honest thought for a moment. "Self Will believed that a man could follow the example of godly people in both their sin and virtue. In other words, you can be saved by doing both."

Great Heart stopped walking and turned to face Honest. "How in the world could he think that? No one would blame him for saying that even the best of godly people have good qualities but are also guilty of sins. The fact is, as believers, we're not expected to live completely free from sin but are required to keep watch and strive to live as free from sin as we can. But if I understand you correctly, this is not what he meant. Rather, he thought pilgrims can live however they want, regardless of whether it is right or wrong."

Honest nodded as they picked the pace back up. "Yes, that's exactly what I meant, and it's what he believed and how he lived his life."

"But how did he support his line of thinking?"

"Why," Honest said, his mouth twisting into a bitter grimace, "he claimed he could back up his lifestyle using Scripture."

"Is that right!" Great Heart said, chuckling rather offensively. "Well, can you be more specific?"

"Let me see if I can explain just as he did," the old man said, thinking back. "Well, for one, he suggested it was acceptable to have affairs with other men's wives since David, God's beloved, had done so. And since Solomon had multiple wives, he could too. He also claimed that lying was permissible since both Sarah and Rahab had done so. Then he went as far as to say that it was acceptable to take things from other people since Jesus told the disciples to go to take a donkey that didn't belong to them." Honest paused and then remembered yet another: "Oh, and one more thing...he said that since Jacob deceived and cheated his father to get the inheritance, then he could too."

The guide closed his eyes and shuddered. "He was a completely depraved man! Are you sure this is what he believed?"

"I'm afraid so," Honest replied. "I've heard him present a defense and argument for this opinion. He even used those Scripture passages to back it up!"

"Well, that opinion shouldn't be allowed anywhere in the world!" Great Heart was emphatic.

"Let me make sure you understand me correctly," Honesty said, as if to clarify. "Mr. Self Will didn't say that *any* person might live this lifestyle; just those who possessed the same virtues of those in Scripture could live this way."

"I can't imagine a more inaccurate interpretation of Scripture," Great Heart said with growing irritation. "He might as well have just said that when godly people sin because of weakness and forgetfulness, they should purposefully continue to live that way without regret. It's like saying a child that gets dirty by stumbling over a rock or by being blown into mud by a strong wind should just willingly lie down and wallow in the mud like a pig. Who would have thought someone could be so blinded by the power of lust? What's written must be true: 'They stumble because they disobey the word, as they were destined to do.'[1]

"His supposing that people addicted to their sins can also have godly virtues is a strong delusion. To eat of the sin of God's people in the same way a dog licks up filth in not a sign of godly virtue.[2] Nor can I believe that anyone that believes this can have faith or love in Christ." Great Heart paused and lifted a brow. "But I'm sure you made strong objections to his opinions. Tell me, what did he have to say for himself when you did?"

Honest grunted in response. "Why, he said to live your life according to your own opinion seemed abundantly more honest to him than to live a life contrary to it."

"A very wicked answer," Great Heart concluded. "It's bad to let our lust freely reign when we know it's wrong, but to advocate for the tolerance of sin is even worse. And to stumble accidentally is also bad, but to fall into the snare intentionally is far worse."

"There are many that think just like him," Honest said pragmatically. "They just don't say it out loud. Unfortunately, though, by their actions, they make going on a pilgrimage seem of little value."

"That's true, and we should grieve deeply over it," Great Heart said, compassion returning to his voice. "But the one who fears the King of Paradise will rise above them all."

Christiana had been listening attentively with eyebrows raised. "There are some strange opinions in this world. I knew someone who once said not to worry because there would be plenty of time to repent from your sin before you die."

"Those types of people are not very wise," said Great Heart. "If that reluctant person had to run a twenty-mile journey in one week to save his life, he wouldn't start the journey until the last hour of the week."

"You're right," Honest assured him. "Yet many of those that consider themselves pilgrims do just that. As you can see, I'm an old man and have traveled this road for a long time and have seen many things. I've watched some set out on their pilgrimage as if taking the world by storm and yet die in the wilderness after only a few days, never seeing the promised land. Then I've seen others who promised nothing when they first set out; you would've thought they wouldn't make it a day, but they have proved very good pilgrims. I've watched some run forward carelessly, who, after just a little time, turned and ran back just as fast. I've also heard some speak positively in the beginning about a pilgrim's life only to speak as strongly against it after a short time. I've heard of some who, when they first set out for Paradise, claimed without question that there is such a place then, when they were almost there, came back again and said that it's not. I've heard some brag about how they would handle themselves if ever opposed but then flee the pilgrim's life completely, even over a false alarm."

Now, as they were on their way, a man came running to meet them saying, "Gentlemen, women, and children, if you love your lives, change direction because there are thieves on the path ahead of you!"

Great Heart's hand went to his sword. "They're probably the three thieves who attacked Little Faith a while back, but we're ready for them."

They continued walking, looking this way and that in case they should run into the villains. But whether they had heard of Great Heart or found someone else to rob, the three thieves never approached the pilgrims.

---

1. 1 Peter 2:8
2. Hosea 4:8

Chapter Twenty-One

Welcomed by Gaius

After traveling for a while, Christiana wished they could find an inn because she and the children had become weary from the day's journey.

"There's an inn not too far from here," Honest said, pointing down the way. "There's a disciple with a good reputation who lives there named Gaius."[1] With the old man's recommendation, they all agreed to head in that direction.

When they arrived at the inn, they went inside without knocking at the door since folks rarely knock at the door of an inn. Then they called for the master of the house and asked if they might stay the night.

Gaius greeted them, smiling warmly. "Yes, you're welcome to stay if you're true believers because my house is only for pilgrims." Christiana, Mercy, and the boys were glad to hear the news of the innkeeper's love for pilgrims. Gaius then showed them to their rooms: one for Christiana, her children, and Mercy and another for Great Heart and the old gentleman.

"Gaius, you've been so good to us, but would you happen to have anything for supper?" Great Heart inquired then gestured at the women and children. "These pilgrims have traveled a great distance today and are exhausted."

Their host looked all too delighted to offer what he had. "It's too late to go out and find food, but what we have you're welcome to, if that will do."

Great Heart graciously accepted the host's generous offer. "We will be content with whatever you have in the house. From my experience, you're never left wanting when you take advantage of what's available."

Gaius went down and spoke to the cook, whose name was Taste-that-which-is-good, with instructions to prepare supper for many pilgrims. After returning, he said, "Come, my good friends. I'm so glad that you're here and that my house can accommodate all of you. While supper is being prepared, let's spend some time learning more about one other, if you don't mind." They all thought that sounded like a good idea and joined him.

Gaius sat down in a large chair and stretched out his legs, his piercing gaze sorting through his guests. "May I ask who the older woman is married to and whose daughter is this younger woman?"

Great Heart leaned back in his own chair and smiled. "The woman's name is Christiana, and she was Christian's wife, a pilgrim from the past. And these are his four children. The younger woman's name is Mercy. She was a neighbor whom Christiana persuaded to join them on their pilgrimage. All the boys wish to take after their father and follow in his footsteps. Their hearts burst with joy anytime they see a place where he slept or even when they find one of his footprints. They're eager to do just as their father did and follow in his path."

Gaius jolted upright, staring at them in amazement. "This is Christian's wife, and these are his children? I knew your husband's father and also his grandfather! Actually, there are quite a few men from his lineage whose ancestors first lived at Antioch.[2] I suppose you've heard your husband talk about them, but his ancestors were very worthy men—worthier than any men I've ever known. They proved to be men of great virtue and courage for the Lord of pilgrims, for His ways, and for those who loved Him."

Their host sat back in his chair again, looking off at nothing in particular. "I've heard stories about many in your husband's family who stood through all kinds of trials for the sake of the truth. One of the first from his family to be tried was Stephen, whom men stoned to death.[3] Then there was James, another from this same generation, who was killed by the sword.[4] This is to say nothing of the trials of Paul and Peter, men of old who were also part of your husband's family. There was also Ignatius, who was thrown to the lions; Romanus, whose flesh they cut off his bones and into pieces; and also Polycarp, a man burned at the stake—and when the flames didn't kill him, they stabbed him to death.

"Then there was another who was hung in a basket in the sun for the wasps to eat and then put in a sack and tossed into the sea to be drowned. It would be utterly impossible to count everyone from that family who suffered injuries and death for the love of a pilgrim's life. And I couldn't be happier to see that Christian left behind four boys as faithful as these. I hope they will carry on their father's good name by following in his steps until they arrive at the same destination he did."

"I think the reality, sir, is that they will do exactly that," Great Heart said, feeling proud of the boys. "They seem sincere in their desire to choose their father's ways."

"I believe it!" Gaius announced enthusiastically. "It's why I say Christian's family is likely to be numerous and spread all over the face of the earth. And for this reason, I think Christiana needs to be looking for young women for her sons to marry. It's important that their father's name and those of his family not be forgotten in the world."

Honest shook his head sadly. "It would be a shame for this family line to end and become extinct."

"It can never end, but it can be diminished," said Gaius thoughtfully. "The only way to maintain this family line is for Christiana to take my advice."

The innkeeper then directed his attention on the boy's mother, who had been contemplating all she had heard. "Christiana, I'm glad to see you and your friend Mercy here together, a lovely couple of women. But if I may offer you some advice, bring Mercy into your family by giving her to your oldest son, Matthew, in marriage. In this way, you will preserve future generations here on this earth." In time, Matthew and Mercy came together as a couple and were married, but we'll talk more about that later.

Gaius now turned the conversation in a new direction. "Let me now speak in support of all women, to remove any disgrace. Just as death and the curse came into the world by a woman, so also did life and health.[5] We must remember, God sent forth His Son, born of a woman.[6] When you read the Old Testament, it's clear how women of the time despised what this first woman did. They desired to have children and happily wondered who the mother of the Savior of the world might be. I will say it again that when the Savior was born, women rejoiced in Him before both man and angel.[7]

"I've never read about a man ever giving so much as one penny to Christ, but the women who followed Him ministered to His needs and gave what they had.[8] There was a woman who washed His feet with her hair and another who anointed His body for burial.[9] It was women who wept when He was going to the cross and women who followed Him from the cross and sat opposite the tomb where they buried Him.[10] It was women who first saw Him on the morning of His resurrection and women who first brought the good news to His disciples that He had risen from the dead.[11] When you consider all of this, it's clear that women have been endowed and pursued with grace and special favor from God and, because of this, share with us in the grace of life."

At this time, the cook sent a message saying that supper was almost ready and to prepare the tablecloth, dishes, salt, and bread.

Matthew rubbed his hands together. "I didn't realize how hungry I was until I saw the tablecloth and heard that supper was ready!"

"In much the same way, all the scriptural truths we learn in this life should awaken our greater desire to sit at the wedding banquet of the King," said Gaius, rising and heading to the table. "In this world, you'll find all manner of preaching, books, and church services, which you can liken to setting a table with dishes and salt. However, none of it will compare to the feast that our Lord will prepare for us when we arrive at His house."

When supper arrived, they first brought out a right-shoulder roast, which was lifted to the Lord in praise. Then they waved a roasted breast before the Lord as an expression of thanksgiving. This was all to remind them that they must begin their meals with prayer and praise to God, much like David praising God by lifting his heart to God while leaning on his harp and playing. Both dishes were fresh and delicious, and they all ate extremely well.[12]

Next they brought out a bottle of wine as red as blood.[13] "Drink freely," Gaius said, lifting a glass in the air. "This is the true juice of the vine that makes the heart of God and man glad." They all drank and were happy.

They next brought out a dessert of crumbled milk. Gaius smiled and motioned to the boys. "Let the boys have it to help them grow."[14]

Then they brought out the next course, a dish of butter and honey. "Eat this freely," said Gaius to his guests. "This is good for comforting your mind and strengthening your judgment. According to Scripture, it was our Lord's dish when He was a child, when it says he will eat butter and honey that He may know to reject evil and choose good."[15]

Next they brought out a dish of tasty apples, which looked very good. Matthew stared longingly at the fruit. "Can we eat these apples since the serpent used this fruit to deceive our first mother, Eve?"

Gaius picked up an apple and examined it closely. "Yes, it's true that the serpent used apples to deceive Eve. But it's sin, not apples, that has defiled our souls. If you eat forbidden apples, you will corrupt your soul, but when we eat apples that are permissible," he said, tossing one to the boy, "it will do you good. Scripture tells us to strengthen ourselves with raisins and refresh ourselves with apples when our love is weak."

Matthew took the apple and looked away. "I only raise this concern because a while back," he said hesitantly, "I got sick from eating fruit."

The guest straightened his back and looked at the boy with an encouraging smile. "Forbidden fruit will make you sick but not fruit that our Lord has allowed."

While they were talking, a dish of nuts arrived at the table. Some at the table began talking about how nuts can ruin fragile teeth, especially the teeth of children.[16]

Gaius heard them talking and said, "In the same way that these nuts are hard and their outer shells keep you from eating them, so it's difficult sometimes to understand Scripture...though it's not meant to rob you of learning." He grabbed a nut and cracked it. "I've brought these here for you to crack and open up the shells to eat what's inside." They all sat around the table happily for a long time, talking about many things.

"My good innkeeper," Honest said, grabbing another nut from the bowl, "while we crack the nuts you gave us, can you please explain this riddle? There was a man whom some consider mad, but the more he gave away, the more he had."

They all paid close attention to see what the good man would say. He sat for a while and then replied, "The one who gives his goods to the poor will have as much again and ten times more."

"I dare say, sir," Joseph said, surprised, "I didn't think you would figure it out."

"Oh, is that right?" said Gaius with a hearty laugh. "Well, nothing teaches quite like experience, and I've been in training for a long time. My Lord has taught me to be kind, and I've found from experience that I've gained because of it. The one who gives freely will grow richer, while another who withholds what he should give becomes poor."[17]

Samuel whispered to his mother, Christiana, "Mother, Gaius is a very good man. Let's stay at this house for a long time and let Matthew marry Mercy before we go any farther."

Gaius, their host, overhead and said, "That's an excellent idea, my child."

They stayed there for over a month, and Mercy and Matthew got married. While there, Mercy, as usual, made coats and garments to give to the poor, which only bolstered the pilgrims' reputation.

But let's once again return to our story. After supper, the younger boys wanted to go to bed because they were tired from traveling. Gaius called to have someone to take them, but Mercy said she would do it and tucked them into their beds, where they slept well. But the rest of the group sat up all night, for they were all enjoying each other's company so much that they didn't want to leave. After talking for a while about the Lord, themselves, and their journey, old Mr. Honest began to nod off.

"What, sir!" said Great Heart, prodding the old man. "Are you getting drowsy? Come now and wake up. I've got a riddle for you."

Having earlier put forth a riddle to Gaius, Honest yawned and sleepily agreed, "Okay, let's hear it."

Great Heart began, "The one who would kill must first be overcome. The one who would live abroad first must die at home."

"Ha!" said Honest. "This is a hard one. It's hard to explain and much harder to do. But come, innkeeper," he said, motioning lazily to his host, "if you don't mind, I'll let you answer it for me. Let's hear what you have to say."

Gaius laughed. "Oh, no! Great Heart gave the riddle to you, and you're expected to answer it."

Honest sat up and rubbed his eyes. He considered the riddle for a moment then happily provided his answer. "Grace must conquer us so that sin can no longer enslave us. And to be a living sacrifice, we must die to self."

"You're correct," Gaius said, obviously impressed with how quickly the old man had solved it. "Both Scripture and experience teach this. For example, until grace displays itself through Jesus Christ and overcomes the soul with its glory, it's altogether impossible to oppose sin. Besides, if sin is Satan's cord by which he binds the soul, how would it be possible to resist before the soul is set free from that affliction?

"Second, whether by reason or grace, no one believes that a man who is a slave to his own sin can be a living testimony of grace. In fact, this reminds me of a story that I think is worth telling you.

"There were two men who went on a pilgrimage. One began when he was young and the other when he was old. The young man had strong natural desires from his life to wrestle with, but the old man's natural desires had weakened over time because of age. The young man walked the same path as the old man and was every bit as free as he. Whose grace do you think shined the clearest since they both seemed so much alike?"

"There's no question that it was the younger man's," said Honest, "because those who face greater opposition in life can provide the best evidence of a strong grace. This is especially true when compared with another whose life has not been half as hard because of old age and diminishing natural desires.

"Besides, I've noticed that old men have made an unfortunate mistake, namely, that they are more likely to deceive themselves into believing they have conquered their natural desires as they've aged. The fact is, old gracious men are the ones best able to offer advice to young men because they've seen how meaningless things are. Even so, if the two were to set out together on a pilgrimage, the younger man would have the advantage of displaying the greatest work of grace simply because the older man's natural desires have declined with age."

They sat talking about these things until the break of the day. By this time, the family was up, and Christiana told her son James to read a chapter; he chose Isaiah fifty-three.

When he finished, Honest asked why the passage said that the Savior was to come up like a root from the dry ground, having no form or majesty that we should look at him and no beauty that we should desire him.

Great Heart considered this before responding, "The first part of your question is referring to the Jews. They are the dry ground from which Christ came. The ground was dry because the Jews themselves were spiritually dry and had lost faith. The second part of your question refers to unbelievers that judge based on outward qualities rather than desiring to see into the Prince's heart. It's like those that don't know that precious stones are covered with a plain outer surface; when they find one, they don't realize what they have and give it away as one might a common stone."

"Well," said Gaius, surveying the group before him, "now that you're here and since, as I know, Great Heart is good with his weapons, after we have refreshed ourselves, let's walk into the fields to see if we can do some good. About a mile from here, there is a giant named Slay Good who causes a lot of problems on the King's highway in these parts and is a master of many thieves. I know his general whereabouts, and it would be good if we could clear him out of these parts."

So they consented and went: Great Heart with his sword, helmet, and shield and the rest with spears and staffs.

---

1. Romans 16:23
2. Acts 11:26
3. Acts 7:59–60
4. Acts 12:2
5. Genesis 3
6. Galatians 4:4
7. Luke 1:42–46
8. Luke 8:2–3
9. Luke 7:37–50, John 11:2, John 12:3
10. Luke 23:27, Matthew 27:55–61, Luke 23:55
11. Luke 24:1, 22–23
12. Leviticus 7:32–34, 10:14–15, Psalm 25:1; Hebrews 13:15
13. Deuteronomy 32:14, Judges 9:13, John 15:5
14. 1 Peter 2:1–2
15. Isaiah 7:15
16. Song of Solomon 6:11
17. Proverbs 11:24, 13:7

Chapter Twenty-Two

Slay Good and Mr. Feeble Mind

When they found Slay Good the giant, he was holding a poor man named Feeble Mind in his hands, whom his servants had captured off the Way. The giant was going through the man's pockets and then intended to pick his bones because he was a flesh-eater.

Slay Good looked out to see Great Heart and his friends at the opening of the cave, holding their weapons. "What do you want?" the angry giant demanded.

"We want you!" Great Heart shouted back, standing firm. His eyes flashed with icy determination. "We've come to avenge the many pilgrims who had courage to resist you but whom you killed after dragging them off the King's highway. Now come out of your cave!"

The giant came out of his cave armed for battle, and immediately the fighting began. They fought for over an hour, stopping only to catch their breath. "Why are you here on my grounds?" Slay Good asked again, this time breathing hard.

"I already told you!" Great Heart snapped back while lifting his sword to attack. "To avenge the blood of pilgrims!"

They began fighting again with the giant gaining ground. Then, with a quick blow, he knocked the brave guide down. Great Heart shot back up just as quickly and, with great determination, attacked Slay Good's head and sides with such power and strength that the giant dropped his weapon. He then struck and killed the giant, cutting off his head and bringing it back to the inn. He also brought Mr. Feeble Mind, the pilgrim, back with him too. Once back, they showed the giant's head to the family then displayed it as they had done others before it as a warning for those that might attempt to do the same in the future.

They all turned their attention to Feeble Mind and asked how he fell into the giant's hands to begin with.

"Well, as you can see, I'm a man in poor health," Feeble Mind stated, fully acknowledging his frail body. "In my hometown of Uncertain, death would knock at my door every day. I thought I would never get well staying where I was, so I left the town where both my father and I were born to become a pilgrim. I've made it this far even though both my body and mind are weak. But I thought, if all I can do is crawl, I will spend my life crawling on the pilgrim's Way.

"When I arrived at the gate at the head of the way, the Lord of that place openly welcomed me. He didn't object to my weak body or my feeble mind. Instead, he gave me everything I needed for my journey, including hope to the very end.

"I was also treated kindly at the Interpreter's house, and his servants carried me up the Hill of Difficulty because they considered it too hard for me. It's true that I've found much relief from other pilgrims, though none were willing to go as slow as I'm forced to go. Still, they would walk up to me and offer me hope and encouragement, telling me it was the Lord's will to comfort the feeble-minded.[1] Then they would continue at their own pace on the Way.

"When I came to Assault Lane and encountered Slay Good, he told me to get prepared to fight. But oh my!" His voice was now quavering. "As feeble as I was, when he took me, I knew I needed help...but I also never believed he would kill me. You see, I didn't willingly go with him into his cave, which is why I believed I would come out alive again. It's because I've heard that not every pilgrim taken captive by violent means will die by enemy hands, especially if God intervenes and he keeps his entire heart focused on his Master.

"Well," he said, pausing long enough to take a breath and then continuing with his story, "it appeared as though the giant would rob me, and that he did. But as you can see, I escaped with my life," he said, holding up his hands and smiling. "And for this I thank my King, who created a plan and you, Mr. Great Heart, as the means through which the plan unfolded. I always keep my eyes open for possible acts of violence. But this I've resolved to know—to run when I can, to walk when I cannot run, and to crawl when I cannot walk. Most importantly, I thank Him who loves me, and I remain fixed on the Way before me. So even though I'm feebleminded, as you can see, my thoughts are on the Celestial City that lies beyond the river with no bridge."

"In your travels, did you ever come across another pilgrim, named Mr. Fearing?" asked old Honest.

"Have I come across him?" Feeble Mind blurted out along with a chuckle. "Yes, of course! He's from the town of Stupidity, just beyond the City of Destruction. Even though it's quite some distance from where I was born, I knew him well because he was my uncle, my father's brother. We both have the same disposition and look alike, although he's a little shorter."

Honest was studying the man closely. "I thought you two might be related. You both have a pale complexion and the same color eyes, and you sound so much alike."

"Others have said the same thing," replied Feeble Mind. "Besides, I also see the similarities."

"Come, sir, and be happy because you're a welcomed guest to me and to my house," said their excellent host, Gaius. "Whatever you need, don't hesitate to ask for it, and my servants will do it gladly."

Feeble Mind smiled courteously. "This is an unexpected favor! It's the sun shining out of a very dark cloud. When Slay Good stopped me and refused to let me go any farther, I don't think he intended to do me this favor! No, I don't think when he was rifling through my pockets that he thought Gaius would end up being my host. Yet here I am!"

As they were talking, a man came running up to the house and called at the door. "About a mile and a half from here, a lightning bolt killed a pilgrim right where he stood. His name was Mr. Not Right."

"Oh my!" cried Feeble Mind, looking astonished. "Is he really dead? Several days back and before I traveled this far, Not Right was keeping me company on the Way. He was there when Slay Good grabbed me, but he quickly escaped. Only it seems he escaped to his death while the giant captured me, and I lived.

"Who would have ever thought the one in the worst condition would have survived and that God would divinely intervene with the weak who are facing certain death and give them life. The giant captured me while Not Right escaped and fled, yet here I am alive, and he is dead."

---

1. 1 Thessalonians 5:14

Chapter Twenty-Three

Good Samaritan's Promise

Around this time, Matthew and Mercy were married, and Gaius also gave his daughter, Phebe, to Matthew's brother James, as a wife. Afterward, they stayed about ten more days at Gaius's house, spending their time and the seasons, like pilgrims usually do.

When it came time to leave, Gaius made them a feast, and they all ate, drank, and were happy. As the hour approached for their departure, Great Heart asked Gaius for the bill to pay for their stay. But Gaius told him it was not customary for pilgrims to pay for their lodgings at his house. Instead, he boarded them by the year but expected to be paid by the Good Samaritan, who had promised to faithfully repay him whatever the charges were when he returned.[1]

Great Heart, overcome with love and appreciation, said to their host, "My dear friend, your faithfulness to both pilgrims and strangers alike bears witness to your loving generosity to the church. I commend you for sending them forward on their journey in pursuit of godly character."[2]

Then Gaius said his goodbyes to all of them, including his children and Mr. Feeble Mind, whom he also gave something to drink for the journey.

As they were heading out the door, Great Heart noticed that Feeble Mind seemed to linger around. "Please come along with us, Mr. Feeble Mind," he said, trying to encourage the man. "I will be your guide, and you will do just as well as the others."

Feeble Mind wriggled uneasily and said somberly, "If only I had a suitable companion! You're all healthy and strong, but as you know, I'm weak. I think it would be best if I follow behind instead of coming with you. That way, if I should begin to suffer from one of my many illnesses, I will not become a burden to both of us. Like I said, I'm a man with a weak body and feeble mind."

He sighed in exasperation and looked away. "Besides, my weakness leads me to become offended by all the things you can easily do but I can't. I don't like laughing, wearing flashy clothes, or speculative discussions. No, I'm such a weak man that I become offended by the things that others feel so at liberty to do. I'm a very ignorant Christian, not yet knowing all the truth. Because of this, it sometimes bothers me when I hear others praising the Lord, because I cannot do the same. I'm like a weak man among the strong or a sick man among the healthy. I feel that I'm so anxiously awaiting misfortune that I don't know what to do next."[3]

"But, brother," said Great Heart, "it's my job to comfort the feebleminded and to support the weak. You really need to come along with us. We will wait for you and lend you our help. For your sake, we will deny ourselves some things, including that which some hold a variety of opinions on or even things that are practical and useful. We will also not enter questionable debates in front of you. We will become all things to you rather than leave you behind."[4]

Now, while they were in the heat of their discussions at Gaius's door, Mr. Ready-to-halt came by with his crutches in his hands as he also was on a pilgrimage.

"How did you get here?" Feeble Mind asked, curiously looking around. "Just now, I complained I didn't have a suitable companion, but then here you are, according to my wish! Welcome, welcome, Mr. Ready-to-halt," he rejoiced, clasping his hands together. "I hope we can help each other along the Way."

"I will be glad to accompany you," the man replied, leaning on a crutch. "And now that we are traveling companions, I will happily lend you one of my crutches."

"No," he said, waving him off, "though I do thank you for your generosity. However, I prefer not to use a crutch until I'm unable to walk properly." Then he smiled and pointing his finger in the air as if to make a point. "But if the occasion arises, I think it may help me against a dog."

Ready-to-halt laughed out loud. "My good man, if either I or my crutches can help you, we're both at your service."

So they all continued their journey. Great Heart and Mr. Honest went first, Christiana and her children were next, and Feeble Mind came walking up behind along with Mr. Ready-to-halt with his crutches.

"Please, sir," said Honest, walking alongside their guide. "Now that we're back on the road, tell us some inspiring stories about others who have gone on pilgrimages before us."

"I'd be happy to," said Great Heart. "I know you've heard how Christian of old met with Apollyon in the Valley of Humiliation and of the difficulties he encountered going through the Valley of the Shadow of Death. I think you've also probably heard how Faithful severely struggled with the likes of Madam Wanton, Adam the first, Discontent, and Shame—four of the most deceitful villains a man could ever meet with on the road."

"Yes, I believe I've heard all these stories," the old man said, nodding his head. "I heard that Faithful's encounter with Shame was the most difficult, but he never grew tired."

"Yes, that's true," said Great Heart. "It's like Christian told him, out of all pilgrims, Shame had the wrong name."

Honest tilted his head to one side. "But where was it that Christian and Faithful met Talkative? Talkative is well known enough but perhaps for the wrong reasons."

"He was a confident fool!" Great Heart said then let out a deep sigh. "Yet many more fools will follow in his ways."

"He almost deceived Faithful with his foolish talk," said Honest.

Great Heart nodded. "Yes, but Christian straightened him out quickly."

They continued walking until they arrived at the place where Evangelist had met with Christian and Faithful and made known what would happen to them at Vanity Fair. Great Heart made a sweeping gesture with his arm. "It was in this area that Christian and Faithful met with Evangelist, who predicted the trouble they would encounter at Vanity Fair."

Honest let out a long whistle as he looked around. "You don't say. I'm sure that was hard information to deliver."

"It was," Great Heart agreed. "Though he provided encouragement at the same time. But now what do we say about these two men? We say they were lion-hearted, with unwavering determination and perseverance. Don't you remember how brave they were standing before the judge?"

"Yes, I remember well," Honest said, thinking back to the stories he'd heard. "Faithful suffered bravely."

"So he did," the guide replied confidently. "But even more brave things happened because of his death, including the conversion of Hopeful and many others!"

Honest prodded their faithful guide. "Please go on! You know these stories better than anyone."

A smile formed at the corner of Great Heart's mouth. "Well, after all of this, Christian left Vanity Fair and encountered By-ends, a very sly man."

"By-ends!" said Honest curiously. "Who was he?"

"He was a mischievous person—a downright deceiver is what he was," said Great Heart. "He pretended to be religious but was actually a very worldly man. He was also very cunning and made sure he would never lose or have to suffer for his deception. Depending on the occasion, he could turn his religion on or off, and his wife was just as good at it as he was. He would shift from opinion to opinion, all along encouraging others to do the same. But as far as I know, he came to a terrible end because of his selfish motives, and no God-fearing person thought very highly of his children."

---

1. Luke 10:34–35
2. 3 John 5–6
3. Job 12:5
4. 1 Thessalonians 5:14, Romans 14:1, 1 Corinthians 8:9–13, 9:22

Chapter Twenty-Four

The Church in Vanity

By this time, they were within sight of the town of Vanity, where they hold Vanity Fair. When they realized how close they were, they discussed how best to pass through the town. Some said one thing and some another.

Finally, Great Heart spoke up. "As you can imagine, I've guided many pilgrims through this town and I'm good friends with an old disciple there named Mr. Mnason, who was born in Cyprus.[1] He will let us stay at his house. If everyone agrees, we will go there." Everyone agreed that was the best course of action and began heading that way.

It was evening before they reached the edge of town, but Great Heart knew the way to his old friend's house. When they arrived, he called out to his friend from outside the door. The old man instantly recognized the sound of his good friend's voice and opened the door to the pilgrims. He greeted them warmly with a smile. "How far have you traveled today?"

Great Heart returned the smile. "We've come all the way from our friend Gaius's house."

"My goodness!" the old man said, motioning them into the house. "You've certainly come a long way and must be exhausted. Please come in and have a seat."

Great Heart embraced his friend. "What a warm welcome, Mnason! Come in, everyone, and find a place to sit. My friend welcomes you all."

"Yes, you are all indeed welcome in my home," he said, greeting each of them as they entered the house. "If you need anything, just ask, and we will do our best to get it for you."

Honest was the first to respond to this generous offer. "Well, for some time, our greatest need has been to find a place to rest and to enjoy good company. Now I hope we have both."

Mnason chuckled and, with his hands, directed their attention to the house. "Well, as for a place to rest...you can see for yourself. But as for good company, I'm sure that will become clear with time and effort."

Great Heart gave Mnason a questioning gaze. "Tell me, are you able to provide lodging accommodations for these pilgrims?"

"Absolutely!" he responded joyfully. "Let me provide you a tour of the house." He first showed the pilgrims to their bedrooms then to a very nice dining room where he said they could visit and dine together before turning in for the night. They were all feeling better after their long journey and took their seats around a large table.

Sitting next to their affable host, Honest began the conversation. "I'm curious, Mr. Mnason. Are there many good people in this town?"

He nodded. "Yes, there are some, but only a few when compared with those who are not."

"Is it possible to go visit some of them?" he asked eagerly. "The sight of good men to those who have been on a pilgrimage is like the moon and stars appearing to those sailing on the high seas."

THE CHURCH IN VANITY

Mnason tapped his foot, and his daughter, Grace, came walking up. "Grace," he said to her, "go tell my friends, Mr. Contrite, Mr. Holy-man, Mr. Love-saint, Mr. Dare-not-lie, and Mr. Penitent, that some friends have arrived at my home this evening and would like to meet them." Grace called on each to see if they could come, and all did. When they arrived and sat down at the table with the others, Mnason introduced each of them to the pilgrims.

"My neighbors," Mnason said with his arms wide before his new guests, "as you can see, I've received a group of strangers to stay in my home. They are pilgrims who have traveled from a long way off and are heading to Mount Zion. But can anyone guess who this is?" he said, pointing to Christiana. "It's Christiana, the wife of Christian, that famous pilgrim who, along with his brother Faithful, this town treated so shamefully."

They were all shocked. "When Grace called on us, we never thought we were coming to meet Christiana. What a wonderful surprise!"

They asked her how she was doing and if these boys with her were Christian's sons. When she told them they were, they said to them, "The King whom you love and serve will make you like your father and will bring you to where he is in peace!"

After they were all seated comfortably around the table, Honest inquired of Mr. Contrite and the others what the current state of the town was.

Contrite raised a critical eyebrow. "You can be sure that during fair time, everyone is in quite the hurry. It's hard keeping your heart and spirit in good working order in such an oppressive environment. Living in a place like this with everything that's going on, you need the spirit to warn you every moment of the day."

"But have your neighbors calmed down any at all?"

He nodded yes. "They're much calmer now than they used to be, when Christian and Faithful were treated so poorly here. So yes, lately I'd say they've been far calmer. I think the blood of Faithful has been weighing heavily on them, and since burning him, they've been ashamed to burn any more. In those days, we were afraid to walk the street, but now we can show our faces. Then to be called a Christian was to be hated. But now, especially in some parts of town—for you know, our town is large—people consider religion honorable."

Mr. Contrite looked around the table at the still weary pilgrims and shifted the conversation back to them. "Please tell us how you have managed on your pilgrimage and how those in other lands treated you."

Honest shrugged. "I guess we managed the best we could and were treated in much the same way as all travelers. Sometimes the Way is easy and other times hard, and we must be careful to watch every step. Frankly, we never know what to expect with any certainty. The wind is not always at our back, nor is everyone a friend whom we meet along the Way. We've experienced considerable difficulties already, and who knows what's yet to come? But we find the old saying mostly true that says a good man must suffer trouble."

"You mentioned difficulties," Contrite commented, keenly interested. "Can you tell us what difficulties you've met with on your journey?"

Honest gestured to Great Heart. "I'll refer that question to our guide as he can give you the best account."

Great Heart leaned in with his elbows on the table. "Well, since leaving, we've been attacked three or four times already. After leaving the gate, two thugs attacked Christiana and her children, and they feared for their lives. Then, along the Way, three different giants attacked us—Grim, Maul, and Slay Good.

"Actually, that's not completely accurate... We attacked the last giant, Slay Good, instead of him attacking us. As it happened, we had been spending time at the house of Gaius, our host. One day the whole church asked if we could take our weapons and go find anyone considered an enemy to pilgrims, most notably a giant we heard lived in the area. Now, Gaius knew this area better than I did because he lived there. So we searched and searched until we finally found the mouth of the giant's cave. This made us happy, and our spirits revived.

"As we approached the cave, it surprised us to find the giant had dragged and forced this poor man," he said gesturing to Feeble Mind, "into his trap and was about to kill him. But when he saw us, he thought he had another prey and left him in a hole to come out and meet us. The battle was intense, and the giant mightily fought back. But in the end, we brought him down to the ground and cut off his head. Then we set it up by the wayside to warn others that would choose to practice such ungodliness. To prove I'm telling the truth, here's the man himself, Mr. Feeble Mind, whom the giant dragged into his cave. He was like a lamb taken out of the mouth of the lion."

Feeble Mind could easily recall the events of that day in his mind. "Great Heart is telling the truth about that day, which was, for me, both disastrous and comforting. It was disastrous when the giant repeatedly threatened to tear me apart but comforting when I saw Great Heart and his friends with their weapons drawing near to save me."

Mr. Holy-man surveyed Great Heart and his fighting pilgrims. "There are two things that one needs to possess for a pilgrimage: courage and a life not stained with sin. If they lack courage, they will never stand firm on the Way. If they're living sinfully, they will make the very name of the pilgrim offensive."

"I hope this warning is unnecessary among all of you," Mr. Love-saint advised. "But unfortunately, there are many who travel that road who would sooner say they don't know what a pilgrimage is rather than acknowledge that there are both unbelievers and believers on the earth."

"It's true," Mr. Dare-not-lie agreed. "They have neither the pilgrim's vigor nor their courage. They refuse to walk morally upright, instead preferring to get their feet all twisted up. One foot turns inward and the other out. As a result, their pants get ripped and torn from falling, all to the disdain of their Lord."

"They should be concerned about these things," said Mr. Penitent, shaking his head. "Pilgrims like this are not likely to receive the grace needed for their pilgrim's progress until such spots and blemishes clear away." They sat around talking and spending time together until the table needed to be set for supper. After eating and refreshing their weary bodies, they went to bed.

They stayed at the fair for a very long time in the house of Mnason. During this time, Christiana's boys grew, and Mnason gave his daughter Grace as a wife to Samuel and his daughter Martha to Joseph.

The pilgrims got to know many of the good people of the town and served them however they could. As usual, Mercy was a testament to her faith, working hard with the poor, who, in turn, blessed her with whatever means they possessed. And truthfully, all the women—Grace Phebe, and Martha—had excellent character and were fruitful in their own respective areas. It was as if Christian's name was once again alive in the world.

While staying there, a monster came out of the woods and killed many of the townsfolk. It would also carry away their children and teach them how to feed on it. Every man in town fled when they heard the monster coming and dared not face it.

The monster was like no other beast on the earth. Its body was like a dragon, and it had seven heads and ten horns. It brought great devastation to the children of the town, and yet there was a woman who controlled it.[2] This monster proposed certain conditions on men, and the men that loved their lives more than their souls accepted these conditions and came under the influence of the beast.

Great Heart, along with those who came to visit the pilgrims at Mnason's house, agreed to engage this monster, thinking they might deliver the people of the town from the paws and mouth of this devouring serpent.

Great Heart, Contrite, Holy-man, Dare-not-lie, and Penitent grabbed their weapons and went forward to meet the monster. At first, it raged and looked with great disdain at its newfound enemies, but the pilgrims, being tenacious fighters and skilled with their weapons, battered the beast about until it retreated. Afterward, they returned home to Mnason's house.

To further clarify, this monster had certain seasons when he came out to make his attempts on the children of the town. During these seasons, these valiant warriors stood watch and continued to assault him. Over time, the monster became not only wounded but lame. Also, he was not ruining the townsmen's children as he once had. Many truly believed this beast would die of his wounds.

In defeating the monster, Great Heart and his fellow pilgrims became famous in the town. Even those considered worldly still highly regarded and respected them. Because of this, the pilgrims suffered very little while in Vanity. It's true, there were some of the more vulgar types that were blind as moles and lacked understanding. They showed no admiration for these pilgrims and disregarded their valor and adventures.

Well, the years passed, and it grew time for the pilgrims to leave. To prepare for their journey, they set aside time to talk with their friends and entrust one another to the protection of their Prince. Those who were able brought such things that were suitable for both women and men to carry and loaded them with enough supplies for their journey.[3] As they set out, their friends accompanied them as far as they could then said goodbye, entrusting them once again to the protection of their King.

---

1. Acts 21:16

2. Revelation 17:3
3. Acts 28:10

Chapter Twenty-Five

Storming Doubting Castle

Great Heart continued leading the pilgrims on the Way, with the women and children struggling to keep up as best they could. Because of their own limitations, Ready-to-halt and Feeble Mind could sympathize with their condition.

No sooner had they left town and wished their friends well than they came to the place where Faithful was killed. They stood there praising God for enabling Faithful to bear his cross so well and for allowing them to benefit from his courageous suffering. Afterward, they continued their long journey while talking of how Hopeful had joined Christian after Faithful's death.

When they arrived at the hill called Lucre, they remembered the story of Demas leaving his pilgrimage for the silver mine, and this is also where some believed By-ends fell and died. They found the old pillar of salt monument standing next to the hill within view of Sodom and its stinking lake. Just like Christian, it amazed them that knowledgeable men with an understanding of sin could be so blinded by greed as to turn aside from the Way. They reasoned that just because someone understands and even witnesses the terrible consequences of destructive behavior doesn't mean their own foolish eyes will not draw them into the same lure of temptation.

I watched as they continued traveling until they came to the river that was on this side of the Delectable Mountains. It was the river where fine trees grow on both sides and whose leaves are good for healing gluttony. It was also the place where the meadows were green all year long and where they could rest safely.[1]

By this riverside in the meadow, there was a sheepfold and a house built for the feeding and teaching of the lambs of those women that were on a pilgrimage. There was One to whom they entrusted the lambs, who took care of them, gathered, and carried them in His arms and would gently lead any that needed help.[2]

Christiana advised her four daughters to commit their little ones to the care of this Man. Their children would live by these waters and receive care, help, and nourishment, ensuring that none would lack in the future. And if any should go astray or get lost, this Man would bring them back again. He would also heal their wounds and strengthen them when sick.[3] In this place, they would never lack food, drink, or clothing and would be safe from thieves and robbers—for this Man will die before losing any of those committed to His trust.

Besides, here they would receive good instruction and training and be taught to walk in the right paths, which is, as you know, no small feat. And there were also delicate waters, pleasant meadows, dainty flowers, and a variety of trees that produce wholesome fruit—not like the fruit Matthew ate that fell over the wall from Beelzebub's garden. This fruit gave health where there was none and continued to increase health where there was. The daughters felt comfortable committing their children to Him knowing that the King was overseeing all of it and there was no better place for children and orphans.

They continued their journey, arriving at By-path Meadow, and saw the fence where Christian and Hopeful crossed over. It was also the place where Giant Despair captured the two men and locked them in the dungeons of Doubting Castle. Knowing this, the pilgrims sat down to discuss the best course of action before going any farther. They were stronger now than before and had Great Heart as their guide. Should they attack the giant and demolish his castle? If they did and were successful, they could set free any prisoners who might be there. It seemed some were for it and others against it. Eventually someone questioned whether it was even legal to travel on ground that was not the King's. Another believed they could as long as everything ended well.

Great Heart had been listening attentively before finally speaking up. "That last reason is not true in every case. However, I have a command to resist sin, to overcome evil, and to fight the good fight of faith. Tell me, with whom should I fight this good fight if not with Giant Despair? Therefore, I will attempt to take his life and demolish Doubting Castle." He stood and issued a challenge to his indecisive companions. "Now, who will go with me?"

"I will," said old Honest, rising to his feet, although slowly due to age.

"And we will too," said Christiana's four sons, Matthew, Samuel, Joseph, and James, for they were now young and strong men.[4]

They left the women on the road along with Feeble Mind and Ready-to-halt with his crutches. Since Giant Despair lived so close, the men were to guard the women until the others returned. But they were to stay on the road because even a little child could lead them.[5]

Great Heart, Honest, and the four young men went up to Doubting Castle to look for Giant Despair. When they arrived and knocked at the castle gate, it made quite an unusual noise.

The old giant heard it and came to the gate with his wife, Diffidence. "Who and what is so brave that they would come and disturb Giant Despair like this?" he fumed as he arrived at the gate, eyeing the intruders.

"It is I, Great Heart," replied the brave guide. "I'm a guide for the King of the Celestial Country and lead pilgrims to their place. I demand that you let me in by opening your gates and preparing to fight. I'm coming to remove your head and demolish Doubting Castle!"

Because he was a giant, Giant Despair believed no man could conquer him. He thought that if in all this time he'd conquered angels, why then should he be afraid of Great Heart? So he equipped himself with his armor and went out to meet them. He wore a cap of steel on his head, a breastplate of fire belted to him, and shoes made of iron, and he held a giant club in his hand.

The six men surrounded him from all sides and began their attack. When his wife, Diffidence, came to help her husband, old Honest cut her down with one blow. They fought for their lives and finally brought Giant Despair down to the ground. But he refused to die. In fact, he struggled hard and seemed to have, as they say, many lives, like a cat. But Great Heart killed him and didn't leave before severing the giant's head from his shoulders.

With Great Despair dead, they easily began to demolish Doubting Castle, which took them seven days to destroy. In the dungeons, they found two pilgrims: Mr. Despondency, who had almost starved to death, and his daughter, Much-afraid. But you can't imagine how many dead bodies were lying around the castle yard, not to mention how full the dungeon was of dead men's bones.

After Great Heart and his companions had performed this great work, they took Mr. Despondency and his daughter Much-afraid, into their protection. They were honest people whom that tyrant Giant Despair had imprisoned in Doubting

Castle. When they had buried the giant's body under a heap of stones, they took his head down to the road and showed their companions what they had done.

One might say that Feeble Mind and Ready-to-halt were delighted, or even ecstatic, when seeing the head of Giant Despair. If requested, Christiana knew how to play the viol and her daughter Mercy could play the lute. Since everyone was so happy, they played them a song, and Ready-to-halt danced. He then took Much-afraid by the hand, and they began dancing in the road. Obviously he couldn't dance without a crutch in his hand, but I promise you, he danced very well. The girl was also to be commended for responding so beautifully to the music.

As for Despondency, he couldn't enjoy the music or dancing because of his hunger from almost starving to death. Christiana gave him some of her bottle of spirits to help him feel better immediately then prepared something for him to eat. In no time, the old gentleman came around, feeling much better.

Now I saw in my dream that afterward Great Heart took the head of Giant Despair and set it on a pole by the side of the highway. He placed it right against the pillar that Christian had erected as a warning to pilgrims that followed him of entering the grounds.

Beneath it he wrote on a marble stone these words: "This is the head of the giant whose name terrified pilgrims in the past. Now his castle is down, and Great Heart has deprived his wife Diffidence of life and saved Despondency and his daughter, Much-afraid. Whoever is reluctant to believe needs to look up here to satisfy all doubts. This head also proved that doubting cripples can dance after being delivered from their fears."

---

1. Psalm 23:12
2. Hebrews 5:12, Isaiah 40:11

3. Jeremiah 23:4, Ezekiel 34:11–16
4. 1 John 2:13–14
5. Isaiah 11:6

Chapter Twenty-Six

The View From the Mountains

After the men had so bravely destroyed Doubting Castle and killed Giant Despair, the pilgrims continued their journey until coming to the Delectable Mountains. This was where Christian and Hopeful had refreshed themselves in the gardens, orchards, vineyards, and fountains. The shepherds were also there to welcome the pilgrims to the mountains, just as they had welcomed Christian.

The shepherds were well acquainted with Great Heart and noticed the large caravan following him. "Great Heart, you've got quite a crowd here!" they said, walking up to meet him. "Tell us, where did you find all of these people?"

The guide nodded a greeting and then cast a quick appraising glance about him. "First let me introduce you to Christiana and her family, including her sons and their wives. Like a vessel, they used their compass to stay on track, steering from sin to grace, or else they would not be here. Next there's old Honest who came on a pilgrimage, and Ready-to-halt, whom I believe to be true at heart. Then there's Feeble Mind, who was not willing to be left behind. And this good man here is Despondency and his daughter, Much-afraid." He then turned his attention back to the shepherds. "Can you offer us accommodations here, or should we travel farther? Please let us know which is best."

The shepherds smiled most welcomingly. "We're comfortable with your companions, and all of you can stay here because we care for the weak and the strong. Our Prince pays attention to everything done to the least of these. Therefore, weakness does not hinder our generosity."[1]

They took them all to the palace door and said, "Come in, Mr. Feeble Mind, Mr. Ready-to-halt, Mr. Despondency, and Mrs. Much-afraid." The shepherds then addressed the guide. "Great Heart, the ones we called in by name are the most likely to draw back. As for you and the rest who are strong, we leave you to your normal freedom."

Great Heart rejoiced at the shepherds' love for his friends. "Today I see that grace shines in your faces and that you are without a doubt my Lord's shepherds. You did not push the diseased and helpless to the side or shoulder but instead scattered flowers on their path into the palace, as you should."[2]

After the feeble and weak went in, Great Heart and the others followed, and all found seats inside. The shepherds then asked those who were weaker, "What is it you would like to have? We structure everything here to support the weak as well as warn the unruly." The shepherds made them a feast that was easy to digest as well as tasty and nourishing. After eating, they all went to rest, with each going to their respective and proper place.

When morning came and the day was clear, the shepherds invited the pilgrims to see some rarities of the nearby mountains, as was their custom. After the pilgrims got dressed and ready for the day, the shepherds took them out into the fields and showed them everything that was shown to Christian.

Then they took them to some new places, beginning with Mount Marvel, where they saw a man in the distance who was moving the surrounding hills with just his words. "What does this mean?" the pilgrims asked, amazed at the sight before them.

"That man is the son of Great Grace, whom you read about in the first part of the records of the Pilgrim's Progress," the shepherds replied. "He's there to teach pilgrims how to believe but also how to remove any difficulties they encounter in life through faith."[3]

Great Heart nodded at the assessment made of the man. "I know him! He's a man above many."

Then they took them to Mount Innocent, where they saw a man clothed all in white. There were two other men there, named Prejudice and Ill-will, who were constantly throwing dirt on the man in white. As the pilgrims watched, the dirt, or whatever they threw at him, fell off just as quickly, leaving his clothes clean. It was like they had thrown no dirt at all.

"What does this mean?" the pilgrims asked curiously.

"The man's name in the white clothes is Godly-man," they replied. "His clothes represent the innocence of his life. Those throwing dirt at him hate his good behavior, but as you can see, the dirt will not stick to his clothes. This is how it is with those living truly innocent in the world. Whoever tries to make such good men dirty just labor in vain. Those who spend a little time with God will cause their innocence to shine forth like a light and their righteousness as the sun at noon."

Then they took the pilgrims to Mount Charity, where they saw a man with a bundle of material lying in front of him. Using the material, he cut out coats and garments for the poor who stood around him. Yet his bundle of material never depleted.

"What does this mean?" they asked the shepherds.

They replied, "This man represents the one who has a heart for the poor and works hard for their benefit. This person will never lack the resources they need. The one who waters will find himself watered. It's like the bread that the widow gave to the prophet. It didn't cause her to have any less oil in her jar."

The shepherds then took them to a place where they saw a man named Fool and another named Want-wit washing an

Ethiopian with dark skin, trying to make him white. But the more they washed him, the blacker he became. Again they asked the shepherds to explain what they were seeing.

The shepherds replied, "What you're seeing represents how a vile person will use every means they know of to gain a good name. But in the end, all their efforts just make them more detestable. This is how it was with the Pharisees and how it will be with everyone who pretends to be religious."

Mercy leaned into her mother-in-law, Christiana, and said in a low voice, "Mother, if possible, I would like to see the hole in the hill that is commonly called the road to hell."

Christiana made the request known to the shepherds, who then took them to the side of that hill and opened the door for Mercy to listen for a while.

As she listened, she heard someone say, "I curse my father for holding me back from the way of peace and life!" Another said, "Oh, if only I was torn to pieces before I lost my soul to save my life!" Then she heard another say, "If I had another chance to live, I would deny myself rather than coming to this place!" Then it was like the very earth groaned and quaked under Mercy's feet. It filled her with fear, and she came away pale and trembling, saying, "Blessed are they who are delivered from this place."

When the shepherds had shown them all these things, they took them back to the palace and showed them as much hospitality as the house could provide. Mercy, though, longed for something that she saw in the house but was ashamed to ask for it.

Christiana noticed her daughter-in-law didn't look well. "Is there something bothering you?" she asked.

Mercy had a soft but strangely agitated expression on her face. "I simply cannot stop thinking about a mirror that's hanging in the dining room. I think if I cannot have it, I will miscarry."

Christiana took the young woman into a motherly embrace. "Let me talk to the shepherds about your desire for the mirror. I'm sure they will not deny you it."

She shook her head. "Then I will be ashamed that these men will know that I've been longing for it."

"No, my daughter," she said with a tender and understanding smile, "there's no shame but only honor in wanting such a thing as that."

"Well then," Mercy said, feeling somewhat better, "will you please ask the shepherds if they will sell it, Mother?"

Now, the mirror was one of a thousand. It could reflect a man's image exactly as he looked with his own features. Then, if the mirror was turned another way, it would reflect the very face and likeness of the Prince of pilgrims Himself. I've talked with those familiar with the mirror, and they've claimed to have seen the very crown of thorns on His head by looking into it. They've also seen the holes in His hands, in His feet, and in His side. This mirror was so extraordinary that it would show the Prince to anyone who had a mind to see Him, whether living or dead, on the earth or in heaven, in a state of humiliation or exaltation, whether coming to suffer or to reign.[4]

Christiana went to the shepherds alone and said, "One of my daughters, who is pregnant, wants something she has seen in this house and believes she will miscarry if you should deny her."

Now, the shepherds' names were Knowledge, Experience, Watchful, and Sincere. With a warm smile, Experience said, "Call her. Please call her. We will absolutely give her what we can."

They called Mercy to them and asked, "Mercy, what is the one thing you desire in this house?"

She blushed, saying, "The large mirror that hangs in the dining room."

Sincere ran and fetched it and, with a joyful blessing, gave it to her. Then she bowed her head and gave thanks. "By your gift, I know that I have approval in your eyes."

They also gave the other young women such things as they desired and then praised their husbands for joining Great Heart in defeating Giant Despair and demolishing Doubting Castle. The shepherds then placed a necklace around Christiana's neck and the necks of her four daughters. They also put earrings in their ears and jewels on their foreheads.

When they were ready to leave, the shepherds let them go in peace but didn't provide the same warnings they gave to Christian and Hopeful when they were there. They didn't need to, since Great Heart was their guide. He was well acquainted with such things and could warn them in a timely manner, even as danger was closely approaching. What warnings Christian and Hopeful had received from the shepherds they had forgotten when the time came to put them into practice. Therefore, this was one advantage this group of pilgrims had over them.

From here they went on singing: "Look how graciously the stage is set for pilgrims to find relief when they come here and how the shepherds received us without one objection and made us feel right at home! They have given us new things so that we might live joyfully and prove that we're pilgrims wherever we go."

---

1. Matthew 25:40
2. Ezekiel 34:21–22, James 1:27
3. Mark 11:23–24
4. James 1:23, 1 Corinthians 13:12, 2 Corinthians 3:18

Chapter Twenty-Seven

Valiant's Zeal for Truth

After leaving the shepherds, they quickly arrived at the place where Christian had encountered Turn-away, who lived in the town of Apostasy.

"This is where Christian met Turn-away, who could not shake his rebellious nature," Great Heart said, reminding them of the story. "Concerning this man, I will tell you he never listened to counsel. Even as he was falling deeper into sin, there was no amount of persuasion that could stop him.

"For example, when he arrived at the cross and the tomb, he met with a man who told him to look at it. Instead, he ground his teeth, stamped his feet, and said he was determined to return home. Even before he came to the gate, Evangelist met with Turn-away and offered to lay hands on him, directing him back to the Way. But he resisted, speaking hatefully to Evangelist before he jumped over the wall and escaped."

The group continued walking, eventually arriving at the place where thieves had robbed Little Faith. They found a man standing there with his sword drawn and his face all bloody. Great Heart placed his own hand firmly on his sheathed sword. "Who are you?" he cautiously inquired of the bruised and beaten traveler.

"My name is Valiant-for-truth," the disheveled man answered. "I'm a pilgrim heading to the Celestial City. As I was traveling on the Way, three men surrounded me and gave me three options: I could either join them, turn around and go home, or die where I stood.[1] I told them I've been true to my faith for a long time, so they couldn't expect me to join up with thieves. Then they demanded I should go home. I told them that was not possible since I had abandoned that life for the Way because I had found it unsuitable and unprofitable. Then they swore I would die. I said my life was valuable and cost far too much to give it away so easily. I then asked them who they thought they were to give me choices to begin with, and if they hindered me in any way, it would be at their own peril.

"Then these three, whose names were Wild-head, Inconsiderate, and Pragmatic, drew their weapons on me, and I also drew mine on them. As you can imagine, the fighting was intense since it was three against one, and it lasted for around three hours." Valiant glanced down at his bruised and bloody body. "And as you can see, they left some marks of their determination on me, but they also took away some of my marks on them. They just now left, perhaps because they heard you coming and ran away."

The man's courage impressed Great Heart. "They stacked the odds against you—three against one!"

"That's true," he agreed but with equal confidence replied, "but numbers don't matter to the one who has truth on his side. It's like the one who said even though my enemy surrounds me, I will not be afraid. Though a war breaks out against me, I will be confident."[2] Valiant shrugged, wiping dirt from the fight off his clothes. "Besides, I've read in some records where one man fought an entire army on his own, and how many did Samson slay with the jawbone of an ass?"

Great Heart cast an appraising glance about the countryside. "Why didn't you cry out for help so that someone might come to your aid?"

"I did," he promptly replied. "I called out to my King, who I knew could hear me and provide invisible help. That was sufficient for me."

"Your behavior is worthy," the guide commended him. "Let me see your sword." Valiant carefully handed it to the guide, who examined the sword in his hands intently. "Ah-ha! It's a legitimate Jerusalem blade."

"Yes, it is," Valiant agreed as Great Heart handed the sword back to him. "Let a man have one of these blades with a hand to wield it and the skill to use it, and he can venture upon an angel with it. He doesn't need to fear holding it if he knows how to use it. Its edges will always be sharp, and it will cut through flesh and bones, soul and spirit, and, for that matter...anything!"[3]

Great Heart studied the tousled man before him. "You fought for a long time. I'm surprised you didn't grow weary."

Valiant stared at the sword still in his hands. "I fought until the sword felt like it was part of my hand. It was as if the two had merged and the sword was growing out of my arm. Then blood ran through my fingers, and I fought back courageously."

"You have done well!" Great Heart said, congratulating him on his victory. "You have resisted to the point of shedding your own blood while striving against sin. We will be your companions, and you can journey with us now." The pilgrims then washed his wounds and gave him what they had to refresh him before continuing on the Way together.

Great Heart was delighted to have Valiant join them because he was good with his hands, especially given the fact that their group was composed of some who were weaker. As they walked, he asked Valiant about many things, including where he was from.

"I'm from Dark Land," Valiant responded. "I was born there, and my father and mother still live there."

"Dark Land!" the guide repeated, along with a sharp glance. "Isn't that town on the same coast as the City of Destruction?"

"Yes, it is," said Valiant and, as if expecting the next question, added, "and I will tell you why I came on a pilgrimage. You see, there was this man named Mr. Tell-true who came into our town, telling us about what Christian had done, specifically, that he left the City of Destruction, leaving behind his wife and children to embrace the pilgrim's life. With confidence, the man reported how Christian killed a serpent that attempted to resist him on his journey but how, in the end, he still reached his intended destination.

"We also heard what a welcome Christian received at his Lord's residence, especially when he came to the gates of the Celestial City, where the angels received him by the sounding of trumpets. He also told us how all the bells in the city rang for joy when Christian entered and how they gave him beautiful clothes to wear. He told us many other things that I will not mention right now. But basically, when True-tale told the story of Christian and his adventures, my heart felt a burning desire to follow him. Both my father and mother wanted me to stay, but I couldn't. So I left them and have come this far on my way."

"You entered at the gate, didn't you?" Great Heart asked, believing he needed to clarify.

Valiant nodded affirmatively. "Oh yes! That same man also told us we must enter at the gate, or it would all be for nothing."

Great Heart turned to face Christiana. "Look at how your husband's story, and all that he received, has spread far and wide."

Valiant quickly turned to face the older woman. "I can't believe it! Is this really Christian's wife?" he asked, surprised.

Great Heart smiled. "Yes, she is." Then he gestured to the surrounding men. "And these are his four sons too."

Valiant was almost speechless. "What? And all are going on a pilgrimage together?"

"Yes, they are truly following in their father's footsteps."

"My heart is so glad!" he said with joyous laughter. "Goodness! Can you imagine how joyful Christian will be when he sees his entire family, who before refused to go with him, now entering the gates after him into the Celestial City?"

"Without a doubt, it will be a comfort to him," Great Heart exclaimed. "For next to the joy of seeing himself there, it will be a joy to be with his wife and children there too."

"As long as you brought it up, I would like to hear your opinion on something," he inquired, turning his attention back to the wise guide. "Some have wondered whether we will know each other in the Celestial City."

Great Heart nodded and paused before he spoke. "Do they think they will know themselves in the Celestial City, and if so, will they rejoice to see themselves in that happiness? And if they think they will know themselves and be happy, why shouldn't they know others and rejoice in their happiness too? And since our families are part of us, even though that relationship will not exist in the same way there, we should wisely conclude that we will be glad to see them there rather than not."

"Well, I think I understand your position on this," said Valiant. Then he returned to their original discussion. "Do you have anything else to ask me about how I first became a pilgrim?"

Great Heart nodded again. "Yes. Did your father and mother want you to become a pilgrim?"

"Oh, no," he said, shaking his head, "they did everything imaginable to persuade me to stay at home."

"Why? What did they have against becoming a pilgrim?"

"They said it was an empty and unproductive life, and if I wasn't so inclined to laziness, I would never consider becoming one."

Great Heart could see where this was going. "What else did they say about becoming a pilgrim?"

"Why, they told me it was dangerous!" he said, his voice rising. "In fact, they said the most dangerous path in the world is the one that pilgrims take."

"Did they explain to you why they thought it was so dangerous?"

"Yes," he replied, "as a matter of fact, they did. They gave me many examples."

"Really!" Great Heart replied, cocking his head to one side. "Can you tell me some of them?"

Valiant didn't hesitate to respond. "Oh, sure! They told me about the Swamp of Despair, where Christian almost drowned. They said there were archers standing ready in Beelzebub's castle to shoot those that knock for entrance at the Wicket Gate. And they also told me about the dark woods and mountains, the Hill of Difficulty, the lions, and the three giants: Grim, Maul, and Slay Good."

He paused only to catch his breath then continued. "Moreover, they said there was a foul fiend that haunted the Valley of Humiliation and had almost killed Christian. They claimed pilgrims must travel through the Valley of the Shadow of Death, where hobgoblins live, where there's no light, and where the Way is full of snares, pits, traps, and altercations. They had heard about Giant Despair and Doubting Castle, not to mention the devastation of pilgrims that found themselves there. In addition, they said I must travel over the Enchanted Ground, which was also dangerous. Then, after all of this, I would find myself at a river with no bridge, which would separate me from the Celestial Country."

Great Heart waited before responding. "Was this all that they said?"

"No," he replied. "They also told me the Way was full of deceivers that laid waiting to turn good men off of the path."

"But how did they know all of this?"

He shrugged. "They heard that Mr. Worldly Wiseman lies along the Way just waiting to deceive pilgrims. Formalism and Hypocrisy are also always on the road, and if I got near By-ends, Talkative, or Demas, they would capture me; if I escaped, Flatterer would surely catch me in his net. Or I would end up following the green path with Ignorance, assuming I was heading for the heavenly gates but instead being led to the hole in the side of the hill and forced to go on the road to hell."

Great Heart's voice was grim. "No doubt that was enough to discourage you. Did their critique of the pilgrim's life end there?"

"Unfortunately, no," he replied. "They also told me of many others in the past who had traveled great distances on the Way, searching for the glory that others had talked so much about. Then these same people would return home, all to the satisfaction of others, feeling foolish for ever stepping one foot out their door and onto that path. They even mentioned several who did so, including Obstinate, Pliable, Mistrust, Nervousness, Turn-away, and old Atheist. There were others, too, who traveled some distance to see what they could find, but none found anything of value."

Great Heart winced at the thought of a parent discouraging their child from becoming a pilgrim. "Did they say anything more to discourage you?"

"Yes," he said, nodding. "They told me about a pilgrim named Mr. Fearing who found the Way so lonely that he never had one hour of comfort. And there was also Mr. Despondency, who almost starved to death on the Way. Oh, and I almost forgot this," he said with a snap of his fingers. "There was once quite the uproar about Christian. Many claimed that after all his adventures to get a celestial crown, it was for certain that he drowned in the Black River, never going a step farther. However, this matter was hushed up."

"And did none of these things discourage you?"

Valiant shook his head and said matter-of-factly, "No. It just seemed like a lot of useless stories to me."

Great Heart smiled a little. "And tell me how you come to this determination."

"Well," he said with a shrug, "I just believed that Tell-true was telling the truth about a pilgrim's life rather than believing a lot of hopeless stories."

Great Heart gave the man a celebratory pat on the back. "Then this was your victory, a wonderful demonstration of your faith."

"Yes, I think so too," Valiant said with a smile. "Because I believed, I became a pilgrim on the Way and have battled everything that would set itself against me. And it's because of this belief that I'm here today."

Great Heart said to the others, "Whoever wants to see true courage should follow the example of Valiant. In doing so, they will remain true regardless of the wind or weather. There is no amount of discouragement that will have them renouncing their faith. Others will become bewildered trying to assail them with dismal stories only to find the pilgrims' faith growing stronger. There's no lion that can scare them, and they'll fight any giant for the right to be a pilgrim. No hobgoblin or foul fiend can daunt their spirit, because they know at the end, they will inherit life. All the delusions of men will pass away, and they will not be afraid as they work night and day to be a pilgrim."

---

1. Proverbs 1:11–14
2. Psalm 27:3
3. Hebrews 4:12

Chapter Twenty-Eight

The Enchanted Ground

By this time, they had reached the Enchanted Ground, where the air naturally tended to make a person drowsy. The ground was all overgrown with briers and thorns except for the few places where there was an enchanted arbor. The arbors were dangerous places where, if a person were to sit or fall asleep, there was some question whether they would wake up again in this world.

The pilgrims traveled through this forest with Great Heart, their guide, leading them and Valiant-for-truth coming up from behind as the rear guard. This was for their safety in case some fiend, dragon, giant, or thief should assault them from behind. Each man walked with his sword drawn in his hand because they knew it was a dangerous place, but they also encouraged one another when they could. Great Heart commanded Feeble Mind to stay near him and placed Despondency under the watchful eye of Valiant.

They hadn't gone too far before a vast, dark fog fell on them. For the longest time, they could barely see one another. The fog was so thick it forced them to feel their way around and call out to one another because they were walking but not by sight. It was clear just how hard it was even for the best of them, but it was even worse for the women and children, whose feet and hearts were tender! Despite the difficulties, Great Heart encouraged them as he led from the front, as did Valiant from the back, and they kept up a pretty good pace.

All the dirt and rock ledges made for difficult terrain, and there wasn't so much as one inn or house to provide food for the weaker pilgrims. This led to a lot of grunting, huffing, and sighing as the pilgrims trekked through the forest. It seemed that when one tumbled over some bush, another would get stuck in the dirt, or some child would lose their shoes in the mud. You would hear one cry out, "I'm down!" and then another would respond, "Hey! Where are you?" Then a third would yell, "The bushes have got such a tight hold on me; I don't think I can get away from it."

Eventually they came to an arbor that looked warm, promising, and refreshing to the pilgrims. The arbor's construction was of fine wrought iron with beautiful greenery overhead, completely furnished with benches to rest and sleep. It also had a soft couch where the weary might lie down. All things considered, you would think this place would be fairly tempting for pilgrims beaten down by the unpleasantness of the path. But not one of them suggested they stop there. From what I could tell, they always listened to the good advice of their guide, who faithfully warned them of imminent dangers. Usually, though, when danger was near, their spirit would stand at the ready, and they would encourage one other to deny themselves. This particular arbor was called the Lazy Man's Friend and was created specifically to lure, if possible, some pilgrims to stop and rest when weary.

Then I saw in my dream as the pilgrims traveled along this lonely road until they came to a place where people are likely to lose their way. When it was light, Great Heart could easily guide the group, helping them avoid paths that would lead them astray, but when it was dark, he came to a standstill. He kept in his pocket a map that showed all ways leading to or from the Celestial City and a box of matches. To see where they were, he struck a match to illuminate the map, which instructed him to be careful and to turn right. Had he not examined the map carefully, they probably would be smothered in mud because just a short distance in front of them, on what seemed to be the cleanest path, there was a pit full of nothing but mud. No one knew how deep the pit was, but it was there to destroy pilgrims.

Then I thought to myself, *Everyone who goes on a pilgrimage needs one of those maps so they can see what direction to take when they are at a standstill.*

They continued journeying through the Enchanted Ground until they came to another arbor built on the side of the highway. There were two men lying in the arbor, named Heedless and Too-bold. These two had made it this far on their pilgrimage, but being tired from their journey, they had sat down to rest and had fallen fast asleep.

When the pilgrims saw them, they stopped, shook their heads, and discussed what to do since the sleeping men were in a critical situation. Should they continue their journey and leave them to sleep, or go try to wake them? In the end, they decided to wake them, if they could. However, they approached with caution and were careful not to sit down or embrace any benefit offered by that arbor.

They went into the arbor and spoke to the men, calling each by his name since Great Heart seemed to know who they were, but they didn't answer. Great Heart shook them and did what he could to wake them.

One of them began to talk in his sleep. "I'll pay you when I get some money." Great Heart just shook his head again.

Then the other said, "I'll fight so long as I can hold my sword in my hand." This made one of the children laugh.

"What is the meaning of this?" asked Christiana.

"They talk in their sleep," said Great Heart. "If you strike them, beat them, or whatever else you do to them, they will answer in the same way. It's like a drunk sailor sleeping on the mast of a ship who's not aware of the waves beating down on him but thinking that whenever he wakes up, he will get another drink.[1]

"You know, when men talk in their sleep, they may say anything, but faith or reason do not govern their words. Their words are as incoherent now as they were before they left on a pilgrimage. This is why arbors are so dangerous. When reckless people like this go on a pilgrimage, the odds are twenty to one that they'll end up behaving this way.

"The Enchanted Ground is one of the last strongholds the enemy uses to entice pilgrims off the Way. Therefore, it's placed almost at the end of the Way to have the best chance against them. For the enemy thinks, 'When will these fools be most likely to sit down? It's when they grow weary toward the end of their journey.' Again, this is why the Enchanted Ground is so near the Land of Beulah and so near the end of their race. Therefore, pilgrims need to examine themselves so the same thing won't happen to them as it did to these that have fallen asleep and can no longer wake up."

Though clearly shaken by the experience, the pilgrims all desired to move forward. However, they asked Great Heart to light a lantern to help them travel the rest of the way by light. The light helped, although the darkness was still very great.[2] But soon the children became exhausted and cried out to Him who loves pilgrims to make their way more comfortable. After going a little farther, a wind arose that drove away the fog, and the air became clearer. They still had quite a distance to travel through the Enchanted Ground, but at least now they could see one another better and the roads they should take.

As they neared the end of the forest, they perceived what they thought was someone engaged in a very serious conversation. As they continued walking toward the sound, they saw a man

THE ENCHANTED GROUND

on his knees with hands and eyes lifted, talking passionately, it seemed, to someone above. They drew closer but couldn't make out what he was saying. So they walked softly until he was done. When the man finished, he got up and began running toward the Celestial City.

Great Heart called after him, "Hello, friend! If you're going to the Celestial City, as it appears you are, why don't you join us?"

The man stopped running and waited for the pilgrims to catch up to him. As soon as Honest was within sight of him, he said, "I know this man!"

"Please tell us, who is he then?" asked Valiant.

"He lived in the same town I did," said Honest. "His name is Standfast, and he's certainly a very good pilgrim."

As they approached one another, Standfast recognized old Honest too and smiled. "Well, hello! Is that you father Honest?"

"Yes, it is I," he acknowledged happily, "just as surely as you are Standfast."

Standfast warmly shook the old man's hand. "I'm so very glad to have found you on this road!"

"And I'm just as glad that I saw you on your knees," he said, nodding in the direction where he saw him praying.

Standfast blushed. "What? You saw me on my knees?"

"Yes, I did," he said approvingly. "And with my all my heart, I was glad to see it."

Standfast wore a puzzled expression. "Why? What did you think when you saw me on my knees?"

"Think!" said old Honest. "What should I think, but that we had found an honest man on the road and would have his company soon?"

"I am happy to know you thought nothing was wrong," he replied then quickly held up a finger. "But had there been, I alone would bear responsibility for it."

"That's true," said the old man, nodding. "But even your concern about that further proves that things are right between the

Prince of pilgrims and your soul because He said blessed is the man who fears sin and its consequences at all times."[3]

Valiant introduced himself to Standfast. "Well, brother, please tell us what caused you to be on your knees just now. Was it for some special compassion or forgiveness that was placed on your heart or what?"

Standfast scanned the horizon as if he were looking for someone. "Well, as you know, we're on the Enchanted Ground. And as I was traveling, I was thinking to myself how dangerous the road was and how many had come this far on pilgrimage only to stop and die here. And then I thought, if they died, how did they die? We know one doesn't die from some violent, painful disease here. In fact, their death isn't even dreadful to them. For the one who dies in their sleep begins that journey with desire and pleasure, submitting to the will of that disease. Well, while I was standing there..."

"Did you see the two men asleep in the arbor?" Honest interrupted, pointing back on the trail.

He nodded. "Yes, I did. I saw Heedless and Too-bold there, and for all I know, they will lie there until they rot.[4] But let me get back to my story."

Standfast recollected his thoughts and continued. "As I said, I was standing there thinking when a woman dressed in old but very nice clothes introduced herself to me. She offered me three things...that is to say, she offered me her body, her money, and her bed. Now, the truth is, I was both weary and sleepy, not to mention poor, and perhaps the witch knew that. Well, I rejected her over and over, but she ignored my rejections and just smiled. Then I began to get angry, but that didn't seem to matter to her at all. She made offers again and said if she could rule me, I would be great and happy. She said, 'I'm the mistress of the world, and I make men happy.'

"I asked her name, and she told me it was Madam Bubble. I tried to get farther away from her, but she still followed me with enticements. Then I fell to my knees, as you saw, with hands raised and crying out, praying to Him who could help me. It was about that same time when you showed up that the woman left. Then I continued to give thanks to the Lord for delivering me. For I truly believe she intended me harm and wanted to stop my journey."

Honest sighed deeply. "There's no question that her plans for you were bad. But wait a second...now that you mention her, I think I've either seen her or read some story about her."

"Perhaps you have done both."

"Madam Bubble!" Honest said as he queried his thoughts. "Is she a tall, beautiful woman with somewhat of a dark complexion?"

"That's right!" he said, quite excited that someone else knew who she was. "You've hit the nail on the head. That's exactly what she looks like."

"And is she also a smooth talker, smiling at you at the end of a sentence?" asked Honest.

"You're correct again because that's exactly what she does."

"Does she wear a great purse on her side, and is her hand often in it, fingering her money as if it were her heart's delight?"

"That's right too!" he said, now beaming. "Had she been standing here right now, you couldn't have more accurately described her features."

"Then the one who drew her picture was a talented artist," said Honest, "and the one who wrote about her told the truth."

Great Heart had been listening to the conversation and decided it was his turn to chime in. "This woman you're talking about is a witch, and it's her evil witchcraft that enchants these grounds. Whoever lays their head in her lap might as well lay it across a chopping block and wait for the ax to drop. She provides a luxurious life for any who look upon her beauty, but they're considered enemies of both God and pilgrims.[5] Yes, she has no doubt bribed many to leave the pilgrim's life and is also a great gossiper. Both she and her daughters are always at the heels of some pilgrim, praising and commending the good things of this life. She's a bold and brazen tramp who will talk with any man. She ridicules and hates poor pilgrims but highly compliments the rich. If she finds one who is cunning at getting money from people, she will speak highly of him everywhere she goes.

"She loves to entertain and feast well, and she's always at one full table or another. In some places, she has made it known that she's a goddess, and some have started worshiping her. At times, she will openly cheat, stating emphatically that no one offers goods that can compare to her own. And if children will love and honor her, she'll promise to live with them. There are even some places and for some people where she will throw out gold from her purse like dust. She loves to be sought after, to be spoken well of, and to lie in the hearts of men. She never tires of praising her wares and loves those most that think the best of her. And for those that will take her advice, she promises crowns and kingdoms to some. Yet she has brought many to the noose and ten thousand times more to hell."

Standfast shook his head as a chill ran down his spine. "Oh, what a mercy that I resisted her! There's no telling where she might have drawn me to."

"Only God knows where she would have drawn you," said Great Heart. "But generally speaking, she would have surely drawn you into many foolish and hurtful lusts, the kind that drown men in destruction and ruin.[6] It was she who set Absalom against his father and Jeroboam against his master. It was she who persuaded Judas to sell his Lord and who prevailed with Demas to forsake the godly pilgrim's life. No one fully knows all the mischief she causes. She brings about conflicts between rulers and subjects, between parents and children, between neighbor and neighbor, between a man and his wife, and between a man and himself, between the flesh and the heart.

Therefore, good Standfast, be as your name is, and when you have done all you can, stand."[7]

As the pilgrims listened to this discussion, there was a mixture of joy and trembling, but eventually they broke out singing: "What danger is the pilgrim in? How many are his foes? How many ways are there to sin? No living mortal knows. Some in the ditch are corrupt and lie rolling around in the mud. Some avoid the frying pan but end up leaping into the fire."

---

1. Proverbs 23:34–35
2. 2 Peter 1:19
3. Proverbs 28:14
4. Proverbs 10:7
5. James 4:4
6. 1 Timothy 6:9
7. Ephesians 6:13

Chapter Twenty-Nine

The Land of Beulah

After this, I watched until they came to the Land of Beulah, where the sun shines night and day. They rested there awhile because they were tired. This country was more familiar to pilgrims, and the orchards and vineyards belonged to the King of the Celestial Country. Because of this, they could make use of anything He had, which refreshed them in no time.

The bells rang and the trumpets always sounded so beautifully that it kept them from sleeping. However, they seemed to stay refreshed, as if they had slept soundly. You could also hear those walking in the streets saying, "More pilgrims have come to town!" Another would answer, saying, "And so many crossed over the water and entered the golden gates today!" Then they would proclaim, "There's a legion of angels that have just come to town. Now we know there are more pilgrims on the road because angels come here to wait on those pilgrims and then to comfort them after all their sorrow!"

The pilgrims got up and walked around town listening to heavenly voices, delighted by all the celestial visions they saw. In this land, they heard nothing, saw nothing, felt nothing, smelled nothing, and tasted nothing that was offensive to their stomachs or minds. It was only when they tasted the river water when it was their turn to cross over that they thought it tasted a little bitter, but it proved sweeter when it was down.

In this place, there was a record kept of the names of past pilgrims and a history of all their famous acts. There was a lot of conversation about the ebb and flow of the river and how it had affected pilgrims who had crossed over. For some it appeared dry, but for others it overflowed its banks.

The children of the town would go into the King's gardens to gather bouquets of flowers and lovingly bring them to the pilgrims. In the garden grew flowers with medicinal benefits, fragrant plants, and saffron, calamus, and cinnamon. There were trees of frankincense, myrrh, and aloes, along with all the finest spices. While they stayed here, the pilgrims' chambers were perfumed and their bodies anointed to prepare them to cross over the river when the appointed time arrived.

While they stayed here awaiting the appointed time, there was talk in town that a messenger had arrived from the Celestial City on a matter of great importance. He was to deliver a message to a woman named Christiana, the wife of Christian the pilgrim. He asked around before being directed to her house.

When the messenger found her, he read the contents of the letter: "Hello, good woman! I bring you greetings that the Master calls for you and expects that you should stand in His presence, clothed in immortality, within the next ten days."

After reading the letter, the courier gave her positive proof he was a true messenger and told her to prepare to leave. The proof was an arrow with a point sharpened with love that passed easily into her heart. Little by little, it worked so effectively with her that when the time came, she had to leave.

When Christiana realized her time had come and that she was the first of her group to cross over, she called for Great Heart, her guide. She told him about the messenger and that she had to leave.

The guide gazed at her tenderly. "Christiana, I'm sincerely happy for you! I couldn't be happier had the messenger come for me."

A slow smile spread over her mouth and spilled into her eyes. "Can you give me some advice about how to prepare for the journey?"

Great Heart told her exactly what to do then added, "Those of us being left behind will accompany you to the riverside."

Christiana called for her children and gave each of them her blessing. "I take comfort knowing the mark of your master is on your foreheads. I'm so glad that you are here with me and have kept your clothes so white." Finally, she gave to the poor what little she had and urged her sons and daughters to be ready when the messenger came for them.

After speaking to her guide and with her children, she called for Valiant. "Sir, you have always shown yourself to be true at heart. Continue to be faithful until death, and my King will give you a crown of life.[1] I would also ask that you keep an eye out for my children. If at any time you see them become weak, please encourage them. My daughters-in-law have been faithful, and when the promise is fulfilled in their own lives, it will be their end."

Then, to Standfast, she gave a ring and afterward called for Honest. "Now, here's a true Israelite in whom there is no deceit," she said when seeing her old friend.[2]

Honest drew close to her. "I wish you a beautiful day when you set out for Mount Zion." Then he added with a wry smile, "And I will be glad to see you cross over the river without getting your clothes wet."

Her laugh was growing weaker. "Whether I'm wet or dry, I just long to be gone. Regardless of how the weather is on my journey, I'll have plenty of time to sit down, rest, and dry off when I get there."

Then came in that good man, Ready-to-halt, to see her. "I know your journey has been difficult," she spoke softly to him, "but it will only make the rest sweeter. Watch and be ready because at a time you're not expecting, the messenger may come for you."

After him, Despondency came in with his daughter Much-afraid, Christiana tried her best to reassure them. "You should always remember with thankfulness your deliverance from the hands of Giant Despair and out of Doubting Castle. It's because of that mercy that you're here safely. Be watchful and alert, casting aside any fear, and remain hopeful to the end."

Feeble Mind was the last to come see her. "You were delivered from the mouth of Giant Slay Good so that you might live in the light of the living forever and see your King with comfort." She slowly reached out, embracing his hand firmly. "Only I would advise you to turn away from your tendency to fear and doubt His goodness before He sends for you. Or else when He comes, you'll have to stand before Him, embarrassed for that fault."

When the day arrived for Christiana to leave, people filled the road to see her take her journey. Amazingly, the banks beyond the river were full of horses and chariots that had come down from above to accompany her to the city gate. She stepped forward and entered the river, saying goodbye to those who had followed her to the riverside. The last words they heard her say were "I come, Lord, to be with you and bless you!" Those who were waiting for Christiana had carried her out of their sight, so her children and friends returned to their homes.

Christiana called at the gate and entered with all the ceremonies of joy that her husband, Christian, had experienced before her. At her departure, her children wept, but Great Heart and Valiant played upon the well-tuned cymbal and harp for joy. Then all went back to their respective places.

1. Revelation 2:10
2. John 1:47

Chapter Thirty

The Pilgrims Receive a Summons

Some time had passed before another messenger came to town, this time to do business with Ready-to-halt. After asking around for him, the messenger found him at his home.

"I've come from the One you have loved and followed, though on crutches," he proclaimed to Ready-to-halt. "God sent me to tell you He expects you to eat at His table in His kingdom the day after Easter, so prepare for your journey." The messenger also gave him proof he was a true messenger, saying, "I broke your golden bowl and snapped your silver cord."[1]

After this, Ready-to-halt called his fellow pilgrims together. "God has sent for me and will surely visit you as well."

He asked Valiant to make his will but only had his crutches and good wishes to leave to those who survived him. "These crutches I leave to my son, who will follow in my footsteps along with a hundred warm wishes he may prove better than I."

He thanked his guide, Great Heart, for his kindness and then prepared for his journey. When he came to the river's edge, he tossed his crutches to the side as he entered the water. "I no longer need these crutches now, since over the river are chariots and horses for me to ride on." The last words they heard him say were "Welcome, life!" And with that, he went on his way.

After this, Feeble Mind was told a messenger was sounding a horn at his door. When the messenger came in, he said, "I've come to tell you that your Master needs you and that in a very short time you will look upon His shining face. Take this as proof of the truth of my message, that those who look out the windows see a dim light."[2]

Then Feeble Mind called for his friends and told them about the message and the proof he had received to confirm it. "There's no reason to make a will since I have nothing to leave anyone," he said, "but as for my weak mind, I'll leave that behind since I have no use for it where I'm going nor is it worth leaving for the poorest pilgrim. Valiant, I would like for you to bury it in animal excrement when I'm gone." Once he had said his piece, the day arrived for him to leave, and he entered the river like the others. Before he crossed to the other side, his last words were "Hold out, faith and patience!"

Some time later, after many of the pilgrims had passed away, another messenger came for Despondency. "Trembling man!" the messenger said with determination in his voice. "The King has summoned you to be ready by the next Lord's Day to shout for joy at your deliverance from all your doubts." For proof of the truth of his message, he gave Despondency the grasshopper to be a burden to him.[3]

When Much-afraid heard what had happened, she wanted to go with her father. So Despondency gathered his friends together and spoke with them about the message he had received. "You know how burdensome the behavior of both my daughter and I has been for every group we have been with. It's our will that our depression and oppressing fears do not pass to anyone else after we depart. Let me be clear: These are spirits that we harbored when first becoming pilgrims. Afterward, we could never shake them. I know that after my death, they will no doubt try to find new pilgrims to offer themselves to. But for our sakes, shut the doors on them!"

When the time came for them to depart, they went to the river's edge and walked in. The last words anyone heard from Despondency were "Goodbye, night! Welcome, day!" His daughter went through the river singing, but no one could understand what she said.

After a while, another messenger came to town inquiring about Honest, eventually arriving where the old man lived. "You're commanded to be ready in one week's time to present yourself before your Lord at His Father's house," the messenger proclaimed, "and the proof of my message is that all the daughters who sing songs will be quiet."[4]

Honest called his friends together to tell them about the message. "I'm about to die but have no plans to make a will," he said matter-of-factly. "As for my honesty, it will go with me. My only request is that you tell my story to all those that come after me."

When the day came to leave, he prepared himself to cross over the river. At that time, the river was overflowing its banks in some places. However, at some point in his life, Honest had spoken to a man named Good-conscience, who had agreed to meet him there and lend him a hand to help him cross over the river. His last words before leaving this world were "Grace reigns!"

After this, there was talk around town that the same messenger who had summoned Honest had summoned Valiant. The proof of his summons to Valiant was that of his broken pitcher at the fountain.[5] When Valiant understood the message, he called for his friends and told them about it.

"I'm going to my Father's," he said, "and even though there was great difficulty throughout my journey, I don't regret any of the trouble I've endured to get to where I am. I leave my sword to the one who will follow me on my pilgrimage and my courage and skill to the one who can get it. I will carry my marks and scars with me to testify to the battles I've fought for Him, who will now reward me."

When the day arrived for his departure, many accompanied him to the riverside. As he walked into the water, he said, "Death, where is your sting?" And as he went deeper, he said, "Grave, where is your victory?"[6] He then passed over with all the trumpets sounding for him on the other side.

Then a summons came for Standfast. This was the man whom the pilgrims had found on his knees in the Enchanted Ground. The messenger brought the summons to him and placed it in his hands, telling him to prepare for a change of life because his Master didn't want him to be so far from Him any longer. Standfast became absorbed in his thoughts, wondering whether the message was true.

Noticing the concern on Standfast's face, the messenger said to him, "There's no need to doubt the truth of my message because here's the proof: The water wheel is broken at the cistern."[7]

Standfast called to their guide, Great Heart. "Sir, although I didn't benefit from being in your company for long during my pilgrimage, it's been to my advantage to have known you. When I left home, I left behind a wife and five small children. When you return—for I know you will return to your Master's house, hoping to guide more pilgrims to this holy place—I ask that you send a message to my family letting them know of all that has happened and will happen to me. Most importantly, tell them of my happy arrival in this place as well as my current blessed condition.

"Also, please tell them about Christian and his wife, Christiana, and how she and her children followed her husband. Tell them about her happy ending and where she is now. I have next to nothing to send to my family unless it is my prayers and tears for them. I would appreciate your telling them this. Perhaps, like Christiana and her family, they will decide to depart on a pilgrimage too."

When Standfast had set things in order and the time arrived for him to leave, he went down to the river. Now, at that time, the river was very calm, and when he was about halfway in, he stood there for a while, talking with his friends who had accompanied him there.

"This river has frightened many people," he said to those on the bank, "and I will admit to being frightened as well. But now I know I'm at peace with it. My feet stand firm on the same ground that the priests stood on while securely holding the ark of the covenant when Israel crossed over the Jordan.[8] The water really does taste bitter and is cold to the stomach, yet the thought of where I'm going and of the transport that waits for me on the other side warms my heart like glowing embers.

"I see that I'm at the end of my journey now, with all my grueling days behind me. I'm going to see that head that was crowned with thorns and that face that was spit upon for me. Until now, my faith has been based on information that I've heard from others, but now I go to where I will live by sight and be delighted just to be in His presence. I always loved to hear people speak of my Lord, and wherever I've seen His footprints on this earth, I've wanted to walk there too. His name has been like an alabaster box containing the sweetest of perfumes. His voice has been most soothing to me, and I've desired His face more than most people desired the sunlight. I used His Word to gather my food and as a cure when I was weak. He has held me and has kept me from my sins, and He has strengthened my steps in His own way."

While he was still speaking, his appearance changed, and the once strong man stooped over and called out, "Take me, for I come to You!" Then suddenly those along the riverbank could no longer see him.

But across the river it was a glorious sight to see—filled with horses and chariots, trumpeters and pipers, and singers and players on stringed instruments, all there to welcome the pilgrims as they went up, following one another into the beautiful gate of the city.

As for Christian's children, the four boys whom Christiana brought with her along with their wives and children, I didn't stay there until they crossed over the river. However, since I left, I have heard someone say they were still alive and would remain where they were for a while, helping grow the church.

If ever I have the opportunity to go that way again, I may give those that want it an account of what I haven't mentioned here. In the meantime, I bid my reader farewell.

The End

---

1. Ecclesiastes 12:6
2. Ecclesiastes 12:3
3. Ecclesiastes 12:5
4. Ecclesiastes 12:4
5. Ecclesiastes 12:6
6. 1 Corinthians 15:55
7. Ecclesiastes 12:6
8. Joshua 3:17

Leave a Review

Thank you again for reading this book! I hope and pray that in some way it encouraged you (and your group) to grow closer to Christ.

If you enjoyed this book, I would appreciate your leaving an honest review for the book and study on Amazon! Your review will help others know if this devotional is right for them.

It's easy and will only take a minute. Just search for "The Pilgrim's Progress, Part 2, Christiana's Journey, Alan Vermilye" on Amazon. Click on the product in the search results, and then click on reviews.

I would also love to hear from you! Drop me a note by visiting me at www.BrownChairBooks.com and clicking on "Contact."

Thank you and God bless!

Alan

The Pilgrim's Progress

A Readable Modern-Day Version of John Bunyan's Pilgrim's Progress

By Alan Vermilye

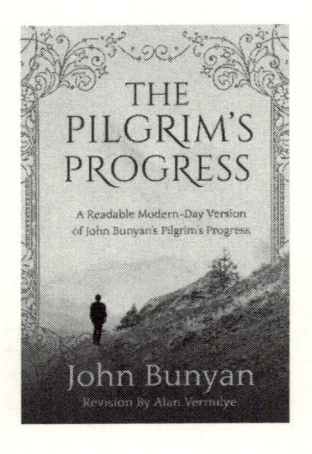

Reading The Pilgrim's Progress by John Bunyan can be a bit challenging even for the best of readers. Not so with this new, easy-to-read version that translates the original archaic language into simple conversational English allowing readers of all ages to easily navigate the most popular Christian allegory of all time.

Without losing any faithfulness to the original text, now you can read Bunyan's timeless classic and reimagine this famous quest that has challenged and encouraged believers for centuries.

What others are saying:

"Phenomenal! Finally able to read The Pilgrims Progress!!!" – Sandra

"What a blessing! Definitely one of the ten books that I have ever read." – TC

"Wow!! This book lights a fire in your heart for sure. Thank you Alan for an accurate revision so that i may understand." – Jesse

"Try reading this book, if you dare. You will find you identify with more than one characters in the book." – Jon

www.BrownChairBooks.com

The Pilgrim's Progress Study Guide
A Bible Study Based on John Bunyan's Pilgrim's Progress
By Alan Vermilye

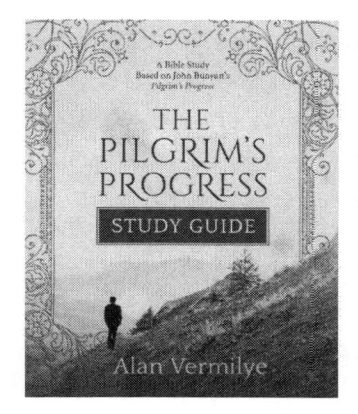

Understanding The Pilgrim's Progress by John Bunyan can be difficult and confusing at times. Not so with The Pilgrim's Progress Study Guide! This comprehensive Bible study workbook will guide you through Bunyan's masterful use of metaphors helping you better understand key concepts, supporting Bible passages, and the relevance to our world today.

Designed to be used alongside The Pilgrim's Progress: A Readable Modern-Day Version of John Bunyan's Pilgrim's Progress, each chapter, sub section, and study question examines Bunyan's allegorical narrative to tell his powerful presentation of what it means to follow the narrow way of Christian salvation.

What others are saying:

"This was a tour de force trip through scripture with rich discussions each week. I highly recommend it!" – Stan

"Invaluable book! My wife and I started rereading The Pilgrims Progress, so I got this study guide, so happy I did! Great study questions yo make you think." – Mark

"I heartily recommend the combination of Pilgrim's Progress and Pilgrim's Progress Study Guide by Alan Vermilye. You'll be glad you took the time to do this study." – Paul

www.BrownChairBooks.com

The Life and Death of Mr. Badman

A Readable Modern-Day Version of John Bunyan's The Life and Death of Mr. Badman

By Alan Vermilye

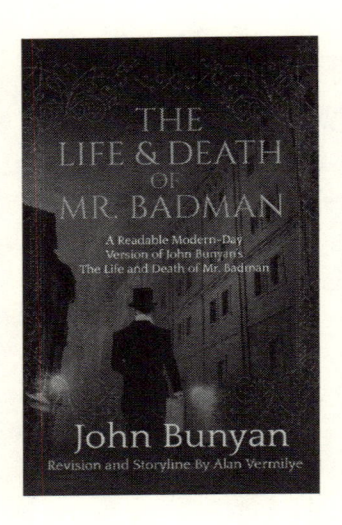

The Life and Death of Mr. Badman by John Bunyan can be a bit challenging, even for the best of readers. Not so with this new, easy-to-read version that translates the original archaic language into simple conversational English, allowing readers of all ages to easily navigate this popular Christian story considered by many to be the third part of The Pilgrim's Progress series.

The Life and Death of Mr. Badman depicts the stages of life—from cradle to grave—of a very wicked man in an evil age and the miserable consequences that undoubtedly follow such wretched living. The book includes the original Bible references and a Bible study guide is available separately for individual and small group use

What others are saying:

"A Very Good Revision Of A Very Badman!!!" – PDT

"This version is much more readable and will no doubt make his story more accessible to modern readers." – MMS

"In a time when many are blind to sin, the book will give an opportunity for them to reflect upon what it means to live a holy, righteous life. Vermilye knocks it out of the park again!" TJ

www.BrownChairBooks.com

The Screwtape Letters Study Guide

A Bible Study on the C.S. Lewis Book The Screwtape Letters

By Alan Vermilye

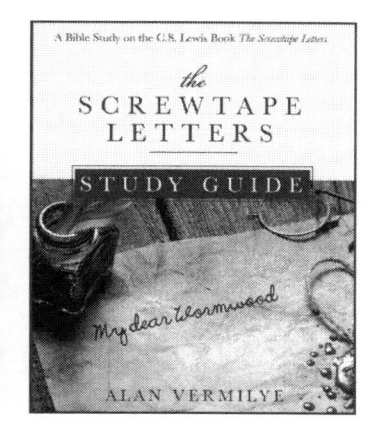

The Screwtape Letters Study Guide takes participants through a study of C.S. Lewis's classic, The Screwtape Letters. This Bible study digs deep into each letter from Screwtape, an undersecretary in the lowerarchy of Hell, to his incompetent nephew Wormwood, a junior devil.

Perfect for small group sessions, this interactive workbook includes daily, individual study with a complete answer guide available online. Designed as a 12-week study, multiple-week format options are also included.

What others are saying:

"This book and study creates a positive reinforcement on fighting that spiritual battle in life. Great read, great study guide!" – Lester

"This study guide was a wonderful way for our group to work through The Screwtape Letters!" – Becky

"Use this study guide for a fresh 'seeing' of The Screwtape Letters!" – William

www.BrownChairBooks.com

Mere Christianity Study Guide

A Bible Study on the C.S. Lewis Book Mere Christianity

By Steven Urban

Mere Christianity Study Guide takes participants through a study of C. S. Lewis classic Mere Christianity. Yet despite its recognition as a "classic," there is surprisingly little available today in terms of a serious study course.

This 12-week Bible study digs deep into each chapter and, in turn, into Lewis's thoughts. Perfect for small group sessions, this interactive workbook includes daily, individual study as well as a complete appendix and commentary to supplement and further clarify certain topics. Multiple week format options are also included.

What others are saying:

"This study guide is more than just a guide to C.S Lewis' Mere Christianity; it is a guide to Christianity itself." – Crystal

"Wow! What a lot of insight and food for thought! Perfect supplement to Mere Christianity. I think Mr. Lewis himself would approve." – Laurie

"Our group is in the middle of studying Mere Christianity, and I have found this guide to be invaluable." - Angela

www.BrownChairBooks.com

The Great Divorce Study Guide
A Bible Study on the C.S. Lewis Book The Great Divorce

By Alan Vermilye

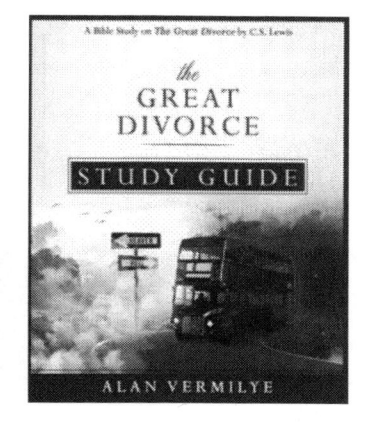

The Great Divorce Study Guide is an eight-week Bible study on the C.S. Lewis classic, The Great Divorce. Perfect for small groups or individual study, each weekly study session applies a biblical framework to the concepts found in each chapter of the book. Although intriguing and entertaining, much of Lewis's writings can be difficult to grasp.

The Great Divorce Study Guide will guide you through each one of Lewis's masterful metaphors to a better understanding of the key concepts of the book, the supporting Bible passages, and the relevance to our world today. Each study question is ideal for group discussion, and answers to each question are available online.

What others are saying:

"To my knowledge, there have not been many study guides for either of these, so to see this new one on The Great Divorce (both electronic and print) is a welcome sight!" – Richard

"I recommend The Great Divorce Study Guide to anyone or any group wishing to delve more deeply into the question, why would anyone choose hell over heaven!" – Ruth

www.BrownChairBooks.com

The Problem of Pain Study Guide

A Bible Study on the C.S. Lewis Book The Problem of Pain

By Alan Vermilye

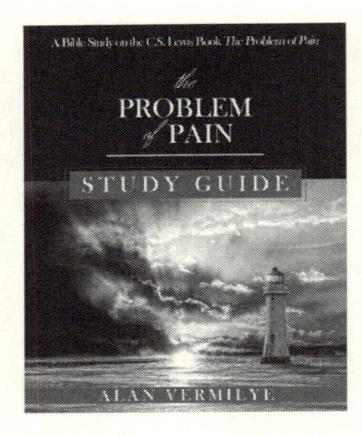

In his book, The Problem of Pain, C.S. Lewis's philosophical approach to why we experience pain can be confusing at times. The Problem of Pain Study Guide breaks down each chapter into easy-to-understand questions and commentary to help you find meaning and hope amid the pain.

The Problem of Pain Study Guide expands upon Lewis's elegant and thoughtful work, where he seeks to understand how a loving, good, and powerful God can possibly coexist with the pain and suffering that is so pervasive in the world and in our lives. As Christ-followers we might expect the world to be just, fair, and less painful, but it is not. This is the problem of pain.

What others are saying:

"Many thanks for lending me a helping hand with one of the greatest thinkers of all time!" – Adrienne

"The questions posed range from very straightforward (to help the reader grasp main concepts) to more probing (to facilitate personal application), while perhaps the greatest benefit they supply is their tie-in of coordinating scriptures that may not always be apparent to the reader." – Sphinn

www.BrownChairBooks.com

The Carols of Christmas

Daily Advent Devotions on Classic Christmas Carols
By Alan Vermilye

The Carols of Christmas is a heart-warming devotional inspired by some of the most beloved Christmas carols of all time. Inside, you'll enjoy a fresh glimpse of some of the same joyful and nostalgic melodies you sing every year now set to personal reflections in this 28-day devotional journey.

The book is divided into four weeks of daily devotions, perfect for celebrating Advent or Christmas. Each week you begin by reading the history of the carol, followed by six daily devotions that reflect on a verse from the hymn along with a Scripture reflection. Traditionally, Advent begins on the fourth Sunday before Christmas, but the devotions are undated, allowing you to start at any time.

What others are saying:

"Well written, joyful, to the point, informative and inspiring. An annual read for Advent from now on. I loved all of it!!!" – Avid Reader

"This was perfect to read and end on Christmas Day! Everyone should read this one." – Janice

"My wife and I read through this Advent devotional this year and found it both interesting and inspiring. Grab one for next year!" – Randy

www.BrownChairBooks.com

The Practice of the Presence of God

A 40-Day Devotion Based on Brother Lawrence's The Practice of the Presence of God

By Alan Vermilye

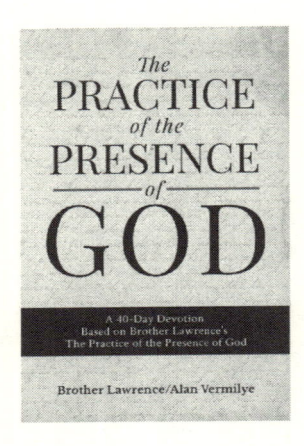

Since it was first published in 1691, The Practice of the Presence of God contains a collection of notes, letters, and interviews given by Brother Lawrence to his friends as a way of helping them turn ordinary daily life events into conversations with God.

Based on this timeless classic, The Practice of the Presence of God: A 40-Day Devotion guides readers on a 40-day journey through the wisdom of Brother Lawrence, related Scripture passages, and devotional thoughts that bring you into a more conversational relationship with God.

What others are saying:

"I love this devotional. It is short and to the point, and thus making it easy to stick to every day!" – Kathleen

"Enlightening new depths in prayer." – Kathy

"This devotional opens the door to Brother Lawrence that brings his letters and conversations to life every day!" – Steve

www.BrownChairBooks.com

It's a Wonderful Life Study Guide

A Bible Study Based on the Christmas Classic It's a Wonderful Life

By Alan Vermilye

It's a Wonderful Life is one of the most popular and heart-warming films ever made. It's near-universal appeal and association with Christmas has provided a rich story of redemption that has inspired generations for decades.

It's a Wonderful Life Study Guide examines this beloved holiday classic and reminds us how easily we can become distracted from what is truly meaningful in life. This five-week Bible study experience comes complete with discussion questions for each session, Scripture references, detailed character sketches, movie summary, and related commentary. In addition, a complete answer guide and video segments for each session are available for free online.

What others are saying:

"Thank you, Alan, for the unforgettable experience. Your book has prompted me to see and learn much more than merely enjoying the film, It's a Wonderful Life." – Er Jwee

"The questions got us all thinking, and the answers provided were insightful and encouraging. I would definitely encourage Home Groups to study this!" – Jill

"It's a Wonderful Life Study Guide by Alan Vermilye is intelligent, innovative, interesting, involving, insightful, and inspirational." – Paul

www.BrownChairBooks.com

A Christmas Carol Study Guide

Book and Bible Study Based on A Christmas Carol

By Alan Vermilye

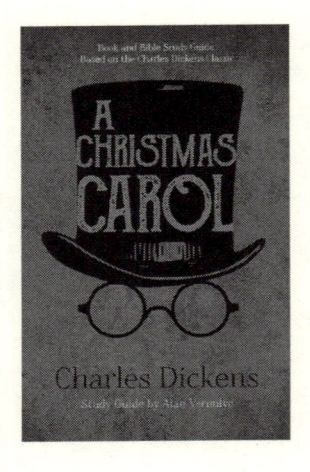

A Christmas Carol Book and Bible Study Guide includes the entire book of this Dickens classic as well as Bible study discussion questions for each chapter, Scripture references, and related commentary.

Detailed character sketches and an easy-to-read book summary provide deep insights into each character while examining the book's themes of greed, isolation, guilt, blame, compassion, generosity, transformation, forgiveness, and, finally, redemption. To help with those more difficult discussion questions, a complete answer guide is available for free online.

What others are saying:

"The study is perfect for this time of the year, turning our focus to the reason for the season—Jesus—and the gift of redemption we have through him." – Connie

"I used this for an adult Sunday School class. We all loved it!" – John

"This study is wonderful!" – Lori

"I found this a refreshing look at the Bible through the eyes of Ebenezer Scrooge's life." – Lynelle

www.BrownChairBooks.com

Made in the USA
Columbia, SC
16 August 2024